Maria Goeppert Mayer

Physicist

Women in Science

Rachel Carson
Author/Ecologist

Dian Fossey
Primatologist

Jane Goodall
Primatologist/Naturalist

Maria Goeppert Mayer
Physicist

Barbara McClintock
Geneticist

Maria Mitchell
Astronomer

Maria Goeppert Mayer

Physicist

Joseph P. Ferry

CHELSEA HOUSE
PUBLISHERS
A Haights Cross Communications Company
Philadelphia

CHELSEA HOUSE PUBLISHERS
VP, New Product Development Sally Cheney
Director of Production Kim Shinners
Creative Manager Takeshi Takahashi
Manufacturing Manager Diann Grasse

Staff for MARIA GOEPPERT MAYER
Editor Patrick M. N. Stone
Production Editor Jaimie Winkler
Photo Editor Sarah Bloom
Series & Cover Designer Terry Mallon
Layout 21st Century Publishing and Communications, Inc.

A Haights Cross Communications ⟍ Company

http://www.chelseahouse.com

First Printing

1 3 5 7 9 8 6 4 2

Library of Congress Cataloging-in-Publication Data

Ferry, Joseph.
    Maria Goeppert Mayer / Joseph P. Ferry.
        p. cm. — (Women in science)
Summary: A biography of Maria Goeppert Mayer, a physicist who contributed to the development of the atomic bomb and who, in 1963, was cowinner of the Nobel Prize in Physics for her work on the nuclear shell model theory. Includes bibliographical references and index.
    ISBN 0-7910-7247-9
    1. Mayer, Maria Goeppert, 1906–1972 — Juvenile literature.
2. Physicists—United States—Biography—Juvenile literature. 3. Women scientists—United States—Biography—Juvenile literature. [1. Mayer, Maria Goeppert, 1906–1972. 2. Physicists. 3. Scientists. 4. Nobel Prizes—Biography. 5. Women—Biography.] I. Title II. Series: Women in science (Chelsea House Publishers)
QC16.M474 F47 2002
520'.092—dc21
                                                    2002015580

Table of Contents

Introduction

Jill Sideman, Ph.D.
President, Association for Women in Science

I am honored to introduce WOMEN IN SCIENCE, a continuing series of books about great women who pursued their interests in various scientific fields, often in the face of barriers erected by the societies in which they lived, and who have won the highest accolades for their achievements. I myself have been a scientist for well over 40 years and am at present the president of the Association for Women in Science, a national organization formed over 30 years ago to support women in choosing and advancing in scientific careers. I am actively engaged in environmental science as a vice-president of a very large engineering firm that has offices all around the world. I work with many different types of scientists and engineers from all sorts of countries and cultures. I have been able to observe myself the difficulties that many girls and women face in becoming active scientists, and how they overcome those difficulties. The women scientists who are the subject of this series undoubtedly experienced both the great excitement of scientific discovery and the often blatant discrimination and discouragement offered by society in general and during their elementary, high school, and college education in particular. Many of these women grew up in the United States during the twentieth century, receiving their scientific education in American schools and colleges, and practicing their science in American universities. It is interesting to think about their lives and successes in science in the context of the general societal view of women as scientists that prevailed during their lifetimes. What barriers did they face? What factors in their lives most influenced their interest in science, the development of their analytical skills, and their determination to carry on with their scientific careers? Who were their role models and encouraged them to pursue science?

Let's start by looking briefly at the history of women as scientists in the United States. Until the end of the 1800s, not just in the United States but in European cultures as well, girls and women were expected to be interested in and especially inclined toward science. Women wrote popular science books and scientific textbooks and presented science using female characters. They attended scientific meetings and published in scientific journals.

In the early part of the twentieth century, though, the relationship of women to science in the United States began to change. The scientist was seen as cerebral, impersonal, and even competitive, and the ideal woman diverged from this image; she was expected to be docile, domestic, delicate, and unobtrusive, to focus on the home and not engage in science as a profession.

From 1940 into the 1960s, driven by World War II and the Cold War, the need for people with scientific training was high and the official U.S. view called for women to pursue science and engineering. But women's role in science was envisioned not as primary researcher, but as technical assistant, laboratory worker, or schoolteacher, and the public thought of women in the sciences as unattractive, unmarried, and thus unfulfilled. This is the prevailing public image of women in science even today.

Numerous studies have shown that for most of the twentieth century, throughout the United States, girls have been actively discouraged from taking science and mathematics courses throughout their schooling. Imagine the great mathematical physicist and 1963 Nobel laureate Maria Goeppert Mayer being told by her high school teachers that "girls don't need math or physics," or Barbara McClintock, the winner of the 1983 Nobel Prize in Medicine or Physiology who wrote on the fundamental laws of gene and chromosome behavior, hearing comments that "girls are not suited to science"! Yet statements like these were common and are made even today.

I personally have experienced discouragement of this kind, as have many of my female scientist friends.

I grew up in a small rural town in southern Tennessee and was in elementary and high school between 1944 and 1956. I vividly remember the day the principal of the high school came to talk to my eighth-grade class about the experience of high school and the subjects we would be taking. He said, "Now, you girls, you don't need to take algebra or geometry, since all the math you'll need to know will be how to balance a checkbook." I was stunned! When I told my mother, my role model and principal encourager, she was outraged. We decided right then that I would take four years of mathematics in high school, and it became my favorite subject—especially algebra and geometry.

I've mentioned my mother as my role model. She was born in 1911 in the same small Southern town and has lived there her entire life. She was always an unusual personality. A classic tomboy, she roamed the woods throughout the county, conducting her own observational wildlife studies and adopting orphaned birds, squirrels, and possums. In high school she took as many science classes as she could. She attended the University of Tennessee in Knoxville for two years, the only woman studying electrical engineering. Forced by financial problems to drop out, she returned home, married, and reared five children, of whom I'm the oldest. She remained fascinated by science, especially biology. When I was in the fourth grade, she brought an entire pig's heart to our school to demonstrate how the heart is constructed to make blood circulate; one of my classmates fainted, and even the teacher turned pale.

In later years, she adapted an electronic device for sensing the moisture on plant leaves—the Electronic Leaf, invented by my father for use in wholesale commercial nurseries—to a smaller scale and sold it all over the world as part of a home nursery system. One of the proudest days of her life was when I received my Ph.D. in physical and inorganic chemistry, specializing in quantum mechanics—there's the love of mathematics again! She encouraged and pushed me all the way through my education and scientific career. I imagine that she was just like the father of Maria Mitchell, one of the outstanding woman scientists profiled in the first season of this series. Mitchell (1818–1889) learned astronomy from her father, surveying the skies with him from the roof of their Nantucket house. She discovered a comet in 1847, for which discovery she received a medal from the King of Denmark. She went on to become the first director of Vassar College Observatory in 1865 and in this position created the earliest opportunities for women to study astronomy at a level that prepared them for professional careers. She was inspired by her father's love of the stars.

I remember hearing Jane Goodall speak in person when I was in graduate school in the early 1960s. At that time she had just returned to the United States from the research compound she established in Tanzania, where she was studying the social dynamics of chimpanzee populations. Here was a young woman, only a few years older than I, who was dramatically changing the way in which people thought about primate behavior. She was still in graduate school then—she completed her Ph.D. in 1965. Her descriptions of her research findings started me on a lifetime avocation for ethology—the study of human, animal, and even insect populations and their behaviors. She remains a role model for me today.

And I must just mention Rachel Carson, a biologist whose book *Silent Spring* first brought issues of environmental pollution to the attention of the majority of Americans. Her work fueled the passage of the National Environmental Policy Act in 1969; this was the first U.S. law aimed at restoring and protecting the environment. Rachel Carson helped create the entire field of environmental studies that has been the focus of my scientific career since the early 1970s.

Women remain a minority in scientific and technological fields in the United States today, especially in the "hard science" fields of physics and engineering, of whose populations women represent only 12%. This became an increasing concern during the last decade of the 20th century as industries, government, and academia began to realize that the United States was falling behind in developing sufficient scientific and technical talent to meet the demand. In 1999–2000, I served on the National Commission on the Advancement of Women and Minorities in Science, Engineering, and Technology (CAWMSET); this commission was established through a 1998 congressional bill sponsored by Constance Morella, a congresswoman from Maryland. CAWMSET's purpose was to analyze the reasons why women and minorities continue to be underrepresented in science, engineering, and technology and to recommend ways to increase their participation in these fields. One of the CAWMSET findings was that girls and young women seem to lose interest in science at two particular points in their pre-college education: in middle school and in the last years of high school—points that may be especially relevant to readers of this series.

An important CAWMSET recommendation was the establishment of a national body to undertake and oversee the implementation of all CAWMSET recommendations, including those that are aimed at encouraging girls and young women to enter and stay in scientific disciplines. That national body has been established with money from eight federal agencies and both industry and academic institutions; it is named BEST (Building Engineering and Science Talent). BEST sponsored a Blue-Ribbon Panel of experts in education and science to focus on the science and technology experiences of young women and minorities in elementary, middle, and high school; the panel developed specific planned actions to help girls and young women become and remain interested in science and technology. This plan of action was presented to Congress in September of 2002. All of us women scientists fervently hope that BEST's plans will be implemented successfully.

I want to impress on all the readers of this series, too, that it is never too late to engage in science. One of my professional friends, an industrial hygienist who specializes in safety and health issues in the scientific and engineering workplace, recently told me about her grandmother. This remarkable woman, who had always wanted to study biology, finally received her bachelor's degree in that discipline several years ago—at the age of 94.

The scientists profiled in WOMEN IN SCIENCE are fascinating women who throughout their careers made real differences in scientific knowledge and the world we all live in. I hope that readers will find them as interesting and inspiring as I do.

The Secret
Revealed

In some sort of crude sense, which no vulgarity, no humor, no
overstatement can quite extinguish, the physicists have known
sin; and this is a knowledge which they cannot lose.
— Physicist J. Robert Oppenheimer,
 on the development of the atomic bomb

As Maria Goeppert Mayer walked along the beach with her
husband and children in Nantucket, Rhode Island one day in
August of 1945, she tried to keep her thoughts far from World
War II and the battles being fought thousands of miles away.
This was their first family vacation since the war began. Maria
wanted only to soak up the warm ocean breezes with the
people who meant the most to her.

As they strolled slowly along the hot, white sand, a
neighbor ran toward them frantically and asked whether
they'd heard the news: the United States had dropped an

The "mushroom cloud" over Hiroshima, Japan, August 6, 1945. The atomic bomb, known informally as "Little Boy," eliminated four square miles of the city and, in conjunction with the bomb dropped on Nagasaki, effectively ended World War II in the Pacific theater. When Maria Goeppert Mayer first heard the news that the United States had dropped the bomb, she despaired—her worst nightmare had come true. Even though she had been on the team that had developed the weapon, she, like several other team members, had always secretly hoped that it would not actually work.

atomic bomb on the Japanese city of Hiroshima.

▼   ▼   ▼

Mayer's connection with the bomb had been three years in the making. In 1942, she had accepted a part-time job teaching science at Sarah Lawrence College in New York. Chemist Harold Urey, who had won a Nobel Prize in 1934, had begun to assemble a secret research group at Columbia University in New York;

the group's mission was to find a way to separate the radioactive element uranium-235, one of the three naturally occurring forms of uranium, from the much more abundant uranium-238. U-235 was fissionable, meaning it could be used to produce nuclear energy; U-238 was not. The group was given a code name: Substitute Alloy Materials, or SAM. The work of SAM was conducted at Columbia, but on behalf of the United States government; its goal was to build the world's first nuclear weapon.

Urey invited Maria Mayer to join the team, and the offer was tempting. At the age of 37, Mayer had earned a reputation in physics and mathematics research, and she wasn't feeling challenged by her teaching job at Sarah Lawrence College. The idea of working full-time worried her, though. Her husband, Joe Mayer, was away in Maryland most of the week investigating conventional weapons at Aberdeen Proving Ground, a military compound, established in 1917, where some 33,000 staff members conducted research on munitions of various kinds.

After giving the offer much thought, Maria told Urey that she would work part-time and never on Saturday, even though most other members of the group worked on the weekend. If one of her children got sick, she told Urey, she would not come to work. To her great surprise, Urey agreed to her terms; he felt she was important enough to the project to merit a little bending of the rules.

As it turned out, Maria Goeppert Mayer's job with SAM developed into full-time work anyway. There were always things that came up, such as reports to write at the last minute. Although she was assigned work that was far from the main line of research, the entire SAM project grew quickly. She had only two or three scientists working under her at the start, but she ended up with over fifty. She thoroughly enjoyed the research and the responsibility, even if she was uncomfortable about contributing to the development of a weapon of mass destruction, one that could have been used on Germany, the country of her birth. "It was the beginning of myself standing on my own two feet as a scientist," she said later, "not leaning against Joe." (Dash, *Triumph*, 294)

The real work of designing the atomic bomb took place at a secret site protected by armed guards and barbed-wire fences in Los Alamos, New Mexico. The facility was in the desert some 35 miles from Santa Fe. It was effectively concealed from the world, which knew nothing of its existence.

Mayer made occasional trips there, and was kept informed of every development, always under the oath of secrecy. When she did see her husband, on Sundays, she had to keep her work to herself. The strain eventually took its toll on her health. She underwent a gall bladder operation and then contracted pneumonia. A thyroid operation followed.

The war in Europe came to an end in the spring of 1945, and at the same time the bomb project neared completion. The whole effort had been complex and costly, but now the bomb was just waiting to be tested.

When Maria visited Los Alamos, the scientists there talked about nothing but the bomb, and by this time she had come to hate being part of the team that had created it. She cringed at the thought of so much destructive power being unleashed on civilians of *any* nation. And she was not alone; in Scotland, Max Born, the hero of her youth, had refused to take part in Britain's atomic bomb project. There were other American scientists who had refused, too, and they were asking the U.S. Secretary of War not to drop the bomb on Japan as planned. They asked that the demonstration of the new weapon take place on an uninhabited island, to prove its might to the Japanese government while avoiding innocent casualties. Their request was not granted; the U.S. government and military and many other scientists were convinced that the bomb had to be dropped— to spare the American lives that would surely be lost in a ground invasion of Japan.

In mid-July of 1945, the world's first atomic device was tested in Alamogordo, a remote section of New Mexico, and the

The testing of the atomic bomb in Alamogordo—the achievement of the Manhattan Project. The project had been a closely guarded secret; Maria Mayer had had to conceal her involvement even from her physicist husband. Despite the campaigning of many important voices in physics, including Max Born, this technology was deployed, and the end for Hiroshima and Nagasaki came only about two weeks after the test.

test was conducted in absolute secrecy. Mayer knew about it but could tell no one, not even her husband.

About a month later the family traveled to Nantucket for the weekend, and Mayer tried to forget, to distract herself.

When the neighbor delivered the news on the beach that morning, Mayer's heart sank. All along, she'd hoped the bomb wouldn't work as planned, or that it would never be needed. She dreaded the thought of thousands, perhaps millions, of people dying slow and horrific deaths from the powerful explosion and subsequent exposure to radiation. Still, she felt a rush of relief. Finally, after all the years of keeping secrets from her family and friends, she could tell the truth about her work on the SAM project.

As they stood on the shore talking, the neighbor turned to Joe and asked whether he'd had anything to do with production of the atomic bomb. The question would stay with Maria for years; both she and her husband were scientists, and both had worked for the war effort, but the neighbor wasn't even considering the possibility that a woman had played a role in developing the bomb. Joe, of course, denied any knowledge, and the neighbor left satisfied.

Maria gently encouraged the children to move ahead as they walked along the beach, so she could let her husband in on the secret she had kept for so long. The words came out quickly, sometimes so fast that they ran together. She had a habit of speaking rapidly when excited. She kept her voice low, but her German accent grew stronger as she finally revealed everything that had built up inside her during three long, difficult years.

Maria watched her children as she spoke. Peter wanted to run back, but his older sister, Marianne, wouldn't let him. Maria knew she could not speak freely with the children around. When she did tell them, she would have to choose her words carefully and speak calmly and reassuringly.

Maria Goeppert Mayer, who later in life would become only the second woman in history to win the Nobel Prize in Physics, had worked on the deadliest weapon ever created. Her dearest friends, the people she admired personally and professionally, had dedicated their lives to it. And she'd hoped it would never succeed.

2

The Early Years: 1906–1927

Science offends the modesty of all real women. It makes them feel as though it were an attempt to peek under their skin—or, worse yet, under their dress and ornamentation!
—Friedrich Nietzsche, 1886

Maria Goeppert (in the German spelling, Göppert) was born on June 28, 1906, in Kattowitz, a German city that is now part of Poland. She was the only child of Dr. Friedrich Goeppert and Maria Wolff.

In 1910 the family moved to Goettingen (or Göttingen), a little medieval town in central Germany, when Dr. Goeppert was appointed Professor of Pediatrics at its university. Goettingen was known throughout the Western world—especially among mathematicians, who considered it the mathematical center of the world—as the location of Georg-August-Universität (Georgia-Augusta University, or

Kattowitz, the city of Mayer's birth, showing the effects of the rapidly advancing technology of the time. The Goeppert family moved to the German city of Goettingen when Mayer was just four years old. She was raised and educated there, enjoying the culture, her family's well-to-do lifestyle, and loving parents. Family friend and physicist Max Born once described the young Maria as "pretty, elegant, a high-spirited lady traveling in the best Goettingen style."

the University of Goettingen). Most people referred to the university by the town's name.

Maria grew up in Goettingen, a festive city alive with students, theater, opera, and concerts, as an only child in a big, comfortable house with lots of servants. There always seemed to be something going on in the Goeppert house, especially lavish dinner parties, for which all the rooms were thrown open and filled with flowers.

Maria's mother had grown up as the oldest of six children in a poor family. Her father had died early and left only a small pension, so she'd been obliged to give piano lessons and teach French to bolster her family's finances. Perhaps because of her humble beginnings, she'd come to feel after her marriage to a university professor that she had to be the best in Goettingen — the best hostess, the best house-keeper, the best mother. At Christmas, she always bought the tallest tree she could find; one year she bought a tree and then saw a taller one, so she returned the first in favor of the second.

Frau Goeppert ran a "formal" house, which meant she required everyone to be on time and to display good manners. The household was run so "formally," in fact, that every once in a while relatives sent their troublesome children there to be taught proper behavior. Maria's mother hovered over her, the couple's only child, like a hen with only one chick to care for.

Despite all the attention from her mother, Maria felt more attached to her father. As a scientist, he was much more interesting to her. He was a huge but gentle bear of a man, warm-hearted and emotionally open. He had started a free clinic for babies and a day nursery for the children of mothers who worked. These children often followed him on the street, waving and calling out as they gathered by his side.

When she was a youngster, Maria's father was her favorite companion. She recalled seeing a half-moon at age three or so, and asking her father what it was. "Any sensible question he would answer," she said. (Dash, *Life*, 237)

When she was seven he prepared special glasses so she

could watch a solar eclipse, and then patiently and carefully explained what was happening. They talked about science during walks together, and went into quarries to collect fossils. They wandered through the countryside learning the trees and plants by name. Sometimes, after a long day at work, he came home and woke his daughter so they could play together. Indeed, the relationship was not typical of German society at the time, for fathers then tended to be distant figures who took no part in the lives of their children. Dr. Goeppert also had an unusual philosophy for raising children: he believed that mothers were the "natural enemy" of their children because they discouraged the children from taking risks.

Moreover, he believed that a mother's natural fear would infect her children. He wanted to see boldness in children, a hunger to learn and to seek adventure; he didn't want to see Maria wasting her life. He disapproved of women who played with their children and had no other interests whatsoever.

Once, when she was about eight, Maria announced to her parents that she would show them how she could climb to the top of a tree in the woods near their home. Before she could grasp the first branch, Maria's father led his wife away. He believed that Maria's mother would have cautioned Maria or even ordered her to come down, had they stayed.

Both her father's academic status and his location at Goettingen had a profound influence on Maria's life and career. She is quoted as saying that her father was more interesting than her mother—for "[h]e was, after all, a scientist." (Dash, *Life*, 237) Her father told Maria that she should not grow up to be a *woman*, meaning a housewife with no larger pursuits. Accordingly, she decided, "I wasn't going to be just a woman." (Dash, *Life*, 238)

Dr. Goeppert's family had produced university professors

going back six generations; and as an only child Maria too would have to become a university professor in order for the tradition to continue. No one said this to her directly, but her duty was understood.

Maria suffered from severe headaches throughout most of her childhood. She had no idea what caused the headaches, which became less frequent and less intense as she got older, just as her father had promised. She had no recollection of any unspoken demands being placed on her, intellectual or otherwise. But she was the kind of child who reacted to anything—to any cold, to any stress—with a headache. They kept her home from school, as did a collection of minor illnesses, for long stretches of time; one year she was allowed to go to school for only two hours each day. Her father warned her against letting this or other pain affect her life too deeply. "If you want to make yourself an invalid, you can," he said. "Don't do it." (Dash, *Life*, 240)

On Maria's eighth birthday, in 1914, Franz Ferdinand, the Archduke of Austria, was assassinated; his death set off the chain of events that led to World War I. The operas and concerts and dinner parties in Goettingen ended abruptly. Food grew scarce, and Dr. Goeppert soon had to find a way to feed not only his own family but also the children he cared for at the clinic.

The food shortage tested Frau Goeppert's ingenuity, too. She arranged all kinds of deals, many of them illegal, just so there would be enough to eat. Sometimes Dr. Goeppert's patients paid him with sausages or other food items. By the time the war was over they were all living on turnip soup, occasionally flavored with a pig's ear—when Maria's mother was fortunate enough to find one.

When the war ended, the Goeppert house once again filled with guests. There were elaborate formal dinner parties for the adults, with the table laid early in the morning so there would be no rush and no hurry. A few years later there were dances for the young people, who danced to music provided by three or four musicians playing the violin and saxophone. Dancing continued long after the musicians left, with Frau Goeppert playing the piano until four in the morning.

THE PATH TO THE UNIVERSITY

At the end of the war, Maria was in her early teens. She began to attend the Hohere Tochterschule, a school for middle-class girls who wanted more out of life than sewing and marriage. The education girls received at these schools was solid; other girls who attended who also went on to make their mark in the world include the nuclear physicist Lise Meitner, whom Albert Einstein called "our Madame Curie"; the mathematician Emmy Noether of Erlangen, who also attended and taught at the University of Goettingen; and Nelly Sachs of Berlin, who won the Nobel Prize in Literature in 1966. Maria—who would win the Nobel Prize in Physics in 1966—was particularly good at languages and mathematics.

In the years after the war, Goettingen's reputation gradually shifted from mathematics to atomic physics—an exploration of the newly discovered and mostly invisible world of the very small. Physicists throughout Europe disregarded national boundaries and came together to work on the theory of the atom as something similar to a planetary system, with electrons orbiting the nucleus. They sought a logical system that would explain the workings of the atoms as clearly and predictably as Isaac Newton had explained the motion of the planets around the sun. Goettingen in the mid-1920s might be described as a "melting pot" of quantum mechanics.

Max Born, one of the atomic physicists who would later refuse to participate in the bomb effort—but who would win the Nobel in 1954 for his research into quantum

Maria's father, Professor Friedrich Goeppert, came from a long line of scientists. Lacking a son to carry on the tradition, he encouraged his only child to continue the family name in academia by studying science. Maria was actually closer to her father than to her mother, a relationship that was atypical in German society at the time, where many fathers were aloof disciplinarians when it came to their children. It was her father who told Maria to be more than "just a woman" and to strive for excellence.

mechanics—joined the faculty at Goettingen in the early 1920s. The Borns and the Goepperts became close friends— so close, in fact, that Maria practically became a member of the Born household. Max Born later remembered the younger Maria as "pretty, elegant, a high-spirited lady traveling in the best Goettingen style." (Dash, *Triumph*, 4) The Goepperts had so many close friends among the mathematicians and physicists that those in the scientific community regarded Maria as a kind of universal niece.

And when the time came for Maria to continue her studies, it was expected, as it always had been, that she would

THE TEACHING CERTIFICATE

Maria Goeppert's interest in mathematics mirrored what was going on in Europe. The reason for the sudden interest in math among female university students could be traced to a newspaper article in the early 1920s that reported a widespread shortage of high school math teachers in schools for girls. Unemployment was high in Germany at the time, and news of the teaching shortage sparked a small group of female mathematicians. Most of them intended to qualify for the teaching certificate rather than for the Ph.D.

For a while, Maria thought she too might leave school after qualifying for the certificate. She attended a few of the required classes in psychology and philosophy, but they were of no use to her. The class in philosophy discussed at length whether or not a dog had a surface—and asked what would become of the surface if the dog were shaved. The psychology class was no better. She attended two lectures and then persuaded her teachers to say she had completed the semester.

In the end, she lost interest in the teaching certificate.

do so at the University of Goettingen. "It somehow was never discussed, but taken for granted by my parents as well as me that I would go to the University," she later wrote. "Yet at that time it was not trivially easy for a woman to do so." (Dash, *Life*, 242) Only about ten percent of the students at most German universities were women. By comparison, about one third of the undergraduate students in the United States were women. Maria was bright and conscientious. Even if she'd had trouble, she wouldn't have hesitated to pull whatever strings were necessary to make it happen.

Maria thought for a time about going into medicine, but her father talked her out of it because he said he always suffered with every child that he lost. "He said it's just too hard," she recalled. "I mean, not too hard physically, but too hard to stand." When she got older, Maria realized her father was right. She knew she didn't have the personality to be a physician.

While Maria idolized her father, she had her mother's temperament. Like her mother, she was generous and loyal, though nervous and quite shy at times—a perfectionist who sometimes demanded more of herself than she was capable of giving.

CHOOSING PHYSICS

She decided to study mathematics because she had a natural talent for it and enjoyed solving problems. This decision proved to be a problem, though, for there was no public institution in Goettingen that prepared girls for this line of study.

In 1921 Maria left the public school to enter a private school, the Frauenstudium, that had been established with the goal of preparing girls for the University's entrance examinations. She was to take part in a three-year program at the Frauenstudium, but the school closed before she could complete her studies. Nevertheless, teachers from the

Family friend Max Born (shown in the background at center) was a professor at the University of Goettingen, where Maria studied. It was Born's influence that inspired Maria to switch her studies from mathematics to quantum physics, a field she found much more exciting. Maria (at the far left) later worked at Goettingen as Born's protégé, and the two remained friends long after they both emigrated to the United States.

Frauenstudium continued their instruction outside of the school, and instead of transferring to a boys' school Maria took the entrance examination as soon as she could.

Called the *Abitur*, the test covered mathematics, French, English, German, physics, history, and chemistry. It took a full week to complete the written examination and a day to complete the oral test. Many people thought Maria was foolish for trying to take the test without completing the preparatory training. They said she was too young, not ready for the challenge. Many even supposed that she would not be allowed to take the test at all. She was, though, and whereas only one of the thirty boys who took the test passed it, all five girls from Maria's school passed.

Maria was admitted to the University in the spring of 1924 as a student of mathematics. Except for one term spent at Cambridge University in England, she spent at Goettingen her entire tenure as a university student. Slim, blonde, and graceful, she became known as the prettiest girl in Goettingen, with a face almost childishly rounded and dreamy. She looked more like a debutante than like the mathematician she hoped to become.

One day in 1927, Max Born invited Maria to join his physics seminar. She joined a group of students who walked in the hills, talked nonstop about physics, and then dined in one of the rustic village inns around Goettingen. Maria found the informal atmosphere and the intensity of her fellow students' discussions exciting. She started thinking that physics may prove a more rewarding career than mathematics. "Mathematics began to seem too much like puzzle solving," she later recalled. "Physics is puzzle solving, too, but of puzzles created by nature, not by the mind of man." (Dash, *Life*, 252)

Maria was still in the Frauenstudium when she had her first taste of atomic physics. She told her parents she was skipping school one day to attend a lecture on recent developments in the atomic world given by their neighbor David Hilbert. "And since I was a brat they let me do it . . . and I learned a lot, and it was very interesting." (Dash, *Life*, 249)

Personal satisfaction was just one reason for changing fields. The shift at Goettingen from mathematics to quantum mechanics—the study of the smallest known particles of matter—was among the greatest intellectual adventures of the first half of the 20th century. Beyond the very small scientific community in Europe, though, quantum mechanics did not cause much of a stir. In America, it was only a rumor: even theoretical physics had hardly been heard of in the United States.

3

Meeting Joe Mayer: 1927–1929

When I was young, seventeen or so, I felt I could understand pretty much how everything worked. . . . My scientific friends have pointed out, well, you didn't know when you were young how everything worked, you didn't know how a cow worked. But I have a fairly good idea *now* how a cow works; whereas the world is getting full of things whose workings hardly anyone can understand or reproduce.

—Joe Mayer

In 1927, soon after Maria switched her studies to physics, her beloved father, Friedrich Goeppert, died. Young Maria and her mother were unprepared for this blow. Nevertheless, Maria vowed to complete her Ph.D. in her father's memory, studying atomic physics under Max Born, and then find a position as a university professor. This last part would be quite a challenge: Goettingen had only one female professor, Emmy Noether,

Joseph E. Mayer, an American chemical physicist (or physical chemist), came to Goettingen because of its growing reputation in the field. Friends told him he should rent a room with the Goepperts because the home was comfortable and Maria Goeppert was the prettiest girl in town. When Mayer met Maria, he found her not only beautiful but also appealingly intelligent. Maria soon felt the same way about him, and the two were married on January 19, 1930.

who was working on invitation for the sheer love of the work; Noether did not receive a salary.

Maria found herself befriending more men than women at the University. She could exchange ideas more easily with men and preferred to discuss work without intimacy.

JOE ARRIVES IN GOETTINGEN

Goettingen's growing reputation as a center for the study of quantum mechanics brought a steady stream of visitors to the campus. One of them was Joseph Edward ("Joe") Mayer, a Canadian-born American who had earned his doctorate at the University of California at Berkeley. Six feet tall, thin, and gangly, Joe was quick-witted and often argumentative. He'd been a thinker since boyhood.

Now, with a year of postdoctoral work under his belt, he was eager to learn about the new field of quantum mechanics; he'd decided to study at Goettingen under James Franck, who was the director of the University's Second Institute for Experimental Physics and a colleague of Max Born. Financed, as many other scientists of the time were, by a grant from the Rockefeller International Education Board, he arrived at Goettingen in the unusually severe winter of 1928–1929.

On arrival, he promptly bought a car. Joe later said he'd had no choice but to buy a car. "I was a Californian," he said. "What does a Californian do without a car?" (Dash, *Triumph*, 6)

The second thing Joe did after arriving in Goettingen was buy a supply of whiskey and gin. Prohibition—legislation banning all alcoholic beverages—was in full swing in the U.S., but there were no such rules in Europe.

The financial disaster that led to the Great Depression still lay in the future for the United States, but Germany was already suffering from an economic downturn, for money had been in short supply since Germany's loss of World War I. Joe's Rockefeller funding made an impression.

Like most other residents of Goettingen, the widowed Frau Goeppert often took in boarders, for the University provided no housing for students or faculty. Joe Mayer went to the Goeppert house almost as soon as he had landed. A friend back home had recommended it as the best place to live because it was comfortable and attractive and contained the prettiest girl in town. All the men were in love with Maria, but most of them had never spoken two words to her. Most were content to simply admire her from afar.

Joe found that the Goeppert house was just as his friend had described it. He fell in love with Maria and set out to win her hand, despite the competition—or perhaps *because* of it. Maria was a challenge. She was dreamy-eyed, delicately built, a terrible flirt, and brighter than any other girl Joe had met.

At first, Maria held back her affection. She liked Joe Mayer and found him attractive, considerate, and funny. She even thought of marrying him. But marriage would mean leaving Goettingen, deserting her mother and her homeland; America was an unknown and frightening world. Still, her chances of becoming a university professor in Germany were slim, and they might be better in the mysterious America.

After a time, Frau Goeppert noticed that her daughter and her boarder were spending a great deal of time together and that Maria was neglecting her schoolwork. "You'd better get married," she told her daughter pointedly, "or you'll never finish up your degree." (Dash, *Life*, 261)

THE DISSERTATION

Maria had completed much of her work on a quantum-mechanical effect in atoms that Max Born had assigned to her as a dissertation problem, but the work still had to be organized and written up. There was also another hurdle: the examination for the degree, the first and last examination required of a German doctoral candidate.

One day, Maria and Joe visited with the physicist Paul Ehrenfest, a theoretician and one of Goettingen's most gifted teachers. Ehrenfest wanted to know how Maria planned to write up her dissertation. He listened intently as she explained her ideas—and then he declared that there was no time to waste. He ordered her upstairs to his office and told her not to come down again until the entire thesis was committed to paper. He locked the door from the outside and left her

Joe and Maria in Joe's car with Frau Goeppert. After they were married, Maria followed Joe to the United States, where he had accepted a faculty position at Johns Hopkins University. However, her hope that it would be easier to gain a professorship in America than in Germany proved unfounded. Instead, she spent most of her professional life working in her husband's shadow.

there until, three hours later, she had completed an outline to his satisfaction.

While Maria had been hesitant in her relationship with Joe, she had no problems with cold calculations. Joe was delighted at the prospect of a wife who was also a scientist, and he vowed to support her wherever she wanted to go. They were married on January 19, 1930 in a ceremony at Goettingen's city hall. After a party at the Goeppert house, they spent their week-long honeymoon at a fashionable hotel in Berlin, where they attended plays and visited Maria's relatives.

After the honeymoon, Maria Goeppert, now Maria Mayer, resumed work on her degree. Writing the thesis took time. On several occasions, both Joe and Frau Goeppert gently pushed her to finish the work. The thesis was devoted to the theoretical treatment of double-photon processes—a photon being a unit of electromagnetic radiation usually used to measure light. Eugene Wigner, with whom Maria would share her Nobel Prize

SCIENTIST OR WIFE?

When Maria Goeppert Mayer started on her scientific career, prejudice against women scientists was so widespread that, until at least the 1920s, a woman who chose a life in physics practically had to renounce the possibility of marriage and motherhood. The possibility of marriage or pregnancy often threatened a female scientist's position, if she could secure one at all, for it was generally assumed that a woman would leave her work, sooner or later, in order to marry. Twenty-three American women worked as physicists in 1921, and, according to a study by Cornell University scholar Margaret Rossiter, not one of them married. "In the 1920s, even some women's colleges would not hire married women. Thus, when Mayer completed her Ph.D. in 1929, a month after her marriage, she became one of the first women to attempt balancing family life and physics."

Nevertheless, as he himself once said, Joe Mayer always thought of her as a wife first.

While at Goettingen, working with Max Born (at right), Maria was one of only two women on the faculty, neither of whom was paid for her services. Maria continued her work there, however, out of a love for the study of atomic physics. Besides that, money in Germany between the wars was in short supply, and universities had little to spend on salaries. Also pictured, at left, is fellow Born protégé Viktor F. Weisskopf, who later became a leading scientist in theoretical physics.

in 1963, once described this thesis as "a masterpiece of clarity and concreteness."

When the thesis was written, there was no way to design an experiment to test the theory it proposed; the technology simply didn't exist. Many years later, though, phenomena of the kind that Mayer was describing would gain importance in the fields of nuclear physics (the study of the nucleus of the atom) and astrophysics (the study of the behavior and physical properties of stars and galaxies). The development of lasers and nonlinear optics has further increased this importance since that time.

When her thesis was almost ready, Mayer faced the examination for her Ph.D. A friend had already failed the experimental part of the test, and this made Mayer worry all the more that *she* would fail, too. When the examination was over, though, they learned that she had passed. Joe invited 40 of Maria's fellow students back to the Goeppert house for brandy, as he'd been prepared to do all along—for he'd never doubted her for a moment.

4

A New Life in America: 1930–1938

If we could produce one or two more Madame Curies, that would accomplish far more for the advancement of women than any amount of agitation, argument, and legislation.
— Educator Virginia Crocheron Gildersleeve,
Many a Good Crusade (1954)

With the examination over and the thesis accepted, Maria's break with Goettingen could be put off no longer. One of her aunts encouraged her to leave, believing that another war in Europe was inevitable and that many people, including Maria's cousins, would die in the conflict.

But Maria did not believe a war was unavoidable. She was not a political person, so she did not understand the implications of the uniformed Nazis who roamed the streets of her hometown. Buried in the physics department by day and either working or dancing with other young scientists at night, she

While at Johns Hopkins, Karl Herzfeld (at right) was a leading scientist in the area of chemical physics. He and Maria's husband at left instructed her in that area of study, thus broadening her knowledge of physics. Maria and Herzfeld would write a number of papers together during her early years at Johns Hopkins, and the two became lifelong friends.

was mostly unaware of what was going on outside of Goettingen. In 1929, when Adolf Hitler was building the foundation for his regime, she knew only that she had pledged her word to live with Joe Mayer in America.

Aside from the upcoming war, there were other reasons for Maria to consider leaving Germany. Although she hoped to become a university professor, she knew it was extremely unlikely in Germany, for women were rare in German university faculties. In America, it might be easier to reach her goal.

So they went, Maria having promised to write to her mother every week and to return home every summer. She knew she would miss her mother terribly, along with the forests, the familiar old town, the food, the language, and the places that held so many fond memories of her father.

When they reached America, Joe accepted an appointment in the chemistry department of Johns Hopkins University in Baltimore, Maryland. Maria found herself having to adapt to a new husband, a new country, and her new professional status. It was not easy.

JOHNS HOPKINS: ON THE OUTSIDE LOOKING IN

To her great dismay—and despite her impressive academic credentials—Maria Mayer was not accepted to the faculty at Johns Hopkins. Instead, she was offered the salary of a few hundred dollars per year to help a member of the science department with his German correspondence.

Still, life at Johns Hopkins wasn't all bad. Mayer would have a chance to do work of her own in a little room in the science building. Her name—or at least the first letter of her maiden name—would be listed in the university catalog. The little money she earned would be enough to pay for a maid when the couple bought a place of their own.

But the administration at Johns Hopkins was not at all interested in quantum mechanics, Mayer's area of expertise. Combined with the lingering effects of the Depression and the university's rule against hiring both members of a married couple, this left her an outsider; and, sure as she was of her abilities as a physicist, she was not prepared for such treatment.

The department at Johns Hopkins wasn't looking for theory at that time; it wanted experimentation and data. Still, one member of the faculty *was* a noted theorist—the Vienna-born physicist Karl Herzfeld, who had arrived at Hopkins from

Munich in 1927. Herzfeld was teaching all the graduate-level courses at Hopkins that dealt with theory, and he was in the vanguard of chemical physics, a very new field of study that combined chemistry and physics. Chemical physics was precisely what Joe Mayer was interested in studying, and he and Herzfeld together drew Maria into the field as well. Chemical physics at the time was feeling the effects of advances that were being made constantly in quantum mechanics, and because Maria's background in quantum mechanics was far superior to that of everyone else at Hopkins, she found herself with unprecedented opportunities to break new ground. Too, her knowledge of chemistry set her apart from many other theoretical physicists of the time, who took great pride in not knowing one chemical compound from another.

She did not limit herself to this one field, though; she took advantage of the various talents existing in the Johns Hopkins department, even spending a brief period working with R.W. Wood, the dean of the Johns Hopkins experimentalists. Another member of the department with whom she had a substantial common interest was the Dutch spectroscopist Gerhard Dieke. She developed particularly close connections with Francis Murnaghan and Aurel Wintner in the mathematics department, which was quite active at that time.

Certainly, though, the two members of the Johns Hopkins faculty who had the greatest influence on Mayer were her husband and Herzfeld; in fact, Herzfeld destabilized the department by lobbying for a full-time faculty position for her. Not only did she write a number of papers with Herzfeld in her early years there; they became close, lifelong friends.

Soon after their arrival in Baltimore, Maria began teaching quantum mechanics to Joe, or at least teaching him the particular approach to quantum mechanics she had learned from Max Born. According to her letters home, the couple quarreled constantly during those teaching sessions, and their fights often ended with Maria in tears. She had no capacity for arguments.

Even so much as a raised voice caused her great stress. Later, Joe said he'd forgotten about the quarrels—and credited his wife with teaching him "all the quantum mechanics I know." (Dash, *Life*, 267)

Meanwhile, Maria was trying to adjust to life in America. She and Joe had rented a tiny row house that was smaller than her dining room had been back in Goettingen. She taught herself to cook and quietly resented the inconvenience of living in a tiny house with no servants. They searched for a car to replace the one Joe had left behind in Germany. Maria wrote home constantly, and read her mother's letters over and over again. When there was too long a wait between letters, Maria would send a cable to her mother. When people asked how she liked America, the best she would do was answer that it wasn't so bad.

She was determined to make the best of her new life because that was her nature and because she felt compelled to justify her decision to leave home. In letters to her mother, she painted glowing pictures of marital bliss. In fact, she missed Germany terribly. She waited anxiously for the ocean liners that brought news and letters from home. Although she had no interest in politics while in Goettingen, she searched the papers for news about German elections. When the Metropolitan Opera performed German works, she sat by the radio and enjoyed the lyrics as much as the music. A German movie, even a bad one, would bring tears to her eyes. "It's terrible but the longer one is away from Germany, the more patriotic one becomes," Maria Mayer wrote in one of her letters to her mother. (Gabor, 118)

With little work to do at Johns Hopkins, Mayer set out to document every detail of her life with Joe in the house on Cresmont Avenue, not far from the campus. No facet of life was too trivial to merit inclusion in her letters home. She described the wallpaper patterns and color schemes she planned for the house. She noted the new bookcases they bought and painted black and white to match their sofa. She reviewed the dances she and Joe attended at the University, complaining at length about the quality of the music.

Perhaps inspired by her mother's thriftiness during the days of surging inflation in Germany, Maria also detailed the family budget. She described how they used the $250 from Joe's monthly salary to pay for household expenses and the $100 or so she received each month to pay off debts. She kept anything that sounded negative out of her letters. Occasionally, she lamented the lack of professional opportunities. Her biggest concern was for her mother's well-being, though.

"You are my only concern," she wrote. "Are you going to concerts at all? Please take care of yourself, and make life a little bit easier for yourself. This is the greatest favor you could do for me." (Gabor, 120)

She spent the summers of 1931, 1932, and 1933 back in Goettingen, where she worked with her former teacher, Max Born. In 1935 she published an important paper that applied techniques she had used for her thesis, but in an entirely different context. At the same time, the return trips to Goettingen helped her to overcome her homesickness. She began to see Germany as old-fashioned and inconvenient, and she became convinced that her aunt had been correct— Germany was headed for war.

Mayer had put off applying for American citizenship, but as the birth of her first child approached she realized she wanted the child to be born of two American parents. At the time, an applicant had to have resided in the U.S. two years before citizenship would be granted; she became a citizen within a few months of learning she was pregnant.

Maria and Joe Mayer's daughter, Marianne, was born in the spring of 1933, just as the Nazi Party, which had just taken over Germany, declared its first racial laws aimed at "cleansing the civil service." (Dash, *Life*, 274) The result was that some 200 Jewish teachers and professors were removed from their posts at Goettingen and sent out of Germany.

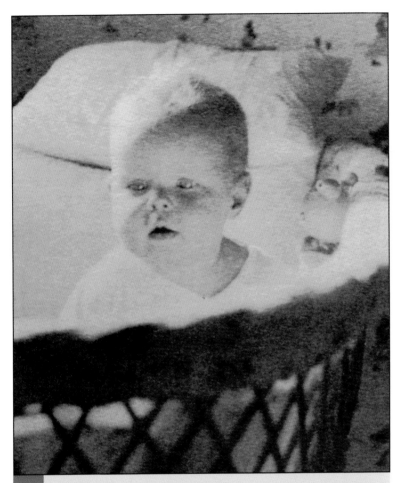

The Mayers' first child, Marianne, was born in 1933. Trying to be a good mother, Maria did less work at the office to spend time with her baby daughter. Later, as Marianne grew older, her mother devoted herself more and more to her work, and the relationship between mother and daughter became distant.

Max Born was among the dozens of Goettingen physicists and mathematicians who left Germany almost immediately. James Franck hoped to remain, believing that the Nazis' power would not last long. Many of the refugees made their way to the United States, and the Mayers opened their home to a seemingly endless stream of visitors. Some stayed for a few days; others stayed for weeks. Some British professors regularly set aside a fixed percentage of their salaries to support exiled German colleagues. Maria and Karl Herzfeld acted as treasurers for the group.

After Marianne's birth, Mayer did very little work in her attic office at Johns Hopkins. She spent most of her time at home, playing with the baby. At the same time, though, she felt a strong desire to return to work, despite feeling a lack of appreciation and recognition at the University. When Marianne was a year old, she returned to her position at Johns Hopkins, which changed little during the nine years she spent there. She never made more than a few hundred dollars a year and never had a voice in university matters or a vote in departmental matters. Her rank remained that of a volunteer associate.

Mayer was simply tolerated at the University, her job seen as little more than a fringe benefit for her husband. Still, the assistantship gave her access to the university facilities, provided her with a place to work in the physics building, and encouraged her to participate in the scientific activities of the university. Joe wanted to fight on behalf of his wife, for he knew she was capable of great work; but she would not allow him to take on the administration.

PERSISTENCE WINS: AWE-INSPIRING LECTURES

In the later years at Johns Hopkins, thanks to sheer tenacity, Maria Mayer earned the opportunity to present some lecture courses for graduate students. She soon proved to be a force to be reckoned with in the classroom: her lectures were dense, streamlined, and highly organized, and she tended to lose no time in explaining background before plunging into the matter at hand. Her ability to manipulate the methods of theoretical physics stunned those in attendance at her courses, and many of her students were in awe of her. They described her as "gracious" and "sympathetic" and able to "speak out, even sharply, but in a quiet way."

To many students, the Mayers were the epitome of a glamorous, modern couple. "Joe and Maria" were both smart and good-looking, always the life of the party. "They were really jazz age types," recalls Robert Sachs, one of Maria's students.

In defiance of Prohibition, the Mayers drank and smoked heavily, but always with style. While others were content with gin made casually in a bathtub, the Mayers crushed grapes for wine using an old washing machine. The couple's legendary

PROHIBITION

Prohibition in the United States was a measure designed to reduce drinking by eliminating the businesses that manufactured, distributed, and sold alcoholic beverages. The 18th Amendment to the U.S. Constitution, passed by Congress in 1917 and ratified by three-fourths of the states in 1919, took away licenses to do business from the brewers, distillers, wine makers, and the wholesale and retail sellers of alcoholic beverages.

The leaders of the prohibition movement were alarmed at the drinking behavior of Americans, and they were concerned that there was a culture of drink among some sectors of the population that was spreading with continuing immigration from Europe.

The prohibition movement's strength grew, especially after the formation of the Anti-Saloon League in 1893. The League and other organizations that supported prohibition, such as the Woman's Christian Temperance Union, soon began to succeed in enacting local prohibition laws. Eventually the prohibition campaign was a national effort.

Prohibition was unpopular and difficult to enforce. The 21st Amendment was passed in 1933, repealing Prohibition, and Americans were once again free to make, sell, and consume alcoholic beverages.

Christmas parties featured delicacies from Germany, lots of alcoholic beverages, and a tree decorated with wax candles. It was the one holiday feast that Maria prepared entirely on her own. The festivities began on Christmas Eve and usually didn't end until the guests finished a huge breakfast of bacon, eggs, and Bloody Marys on Christmas morning.

Although she taught some of the most difficult and complicated courses at Johns Hopkins, Maria never received a professor's salary. During the 1930s, she taught more than half a dozen courses in the university's physics department, including statistical mechanics (the laws that govern the assemblies of molecules), quantum statistics (statistics that deal with the distribution of a particular type of elementary particle among distinct energy states), and classical mechanics (motion and the forces that cause it). The most she was ever paid was $200 a year, about one tenth of the salary earned by male professors of rank similar to her own, volunteer associate. In 1935, four years into her teaching career at Johns Hopkins, the administration seriously considered eliminating even that small token payment.

Angered by the lack of respect for a valued colleague, Karl Herzfeld sent a letter to university president Joseph Ames in Maria Mayer's defense:

> Let me take this occasion to state that in my opinion [Mayer] does at least one third of the work of a full time associate, both as a teacher and in research. She teaches usually two hours for half a year, an advanced course in theoretical physics, and is besides active, on equal footing with Dieke and myself, in two seminars throughout the year.
>
> In addition, she gives, together with her husband and Dr. Andrews, a two hour seminar in chemistry throughout the year. So far as her research is concerned, she publishes several papers a year, usually in conjunction with [Joe]

Mayer or myself. . . . In conclusion, I think she is a very
valuable member of the department, both as a teacher and
as far as the publications emanating from the department
go. From the estimate made before, the adequate amount
of remuneration would be $1,000. (Gabor, 124)

Herzfeld's letter earned Mayer a temporary reprieve, but
although she didn't have her salary cut, she didn't receive a
raise, either. In fact, she had resigned herself to tiny paychecks.
"The university has so little money that I'm always afraid that
it will wind up going bankrupt," she wrote in a letter to her
mother. (Gabor, 124)

By the mid-1930s, Mayer began to realize the importance
of her work. In another letter to her mother, she said the
lectures were more fun. "I don't need to prepare as much, and
they are much less tiring," she wrote.

It was becoming clearer and clearer to Joe Mayer that
Maria needed to forge a serious career in physics. He had
married her as a fellow scientist and saw no reason for her
to become anything else, for he loved science and wanted
his spouse to share the passion. By being married to a fellow
scientist, Joe thought he could avoid many distractions, such as
coming home from work and facing a protracted description of
what his children had done during the day.

Even without Joe's active encouragement, Maria probably
would have plunged fully into her profession eventually.
Whether she could have succeeded without his encouragement
is another matter.

In her later years at Johns Hopkins, Maria met Edward Teller,
who would later be known as "the father of the hydrogen bomb."
Teller had come to the United States from Hungary with a
passion for physics. He worked at George Washington University
in Washington, D.C. and paid regular visits to Johns Hopkins. In
Mayer, Teller found someone anxious to learn about the latest
developments in theoretical physics (theory or speculation rather

Edward Teller was a charismatic and enthusiastic physics professor when Maria first met him at Johns Hopkins. Both he and Maria were interested in atomic physics, and he became a mentor to her. Later, Teller, who was Maria's boss when she headed the Opacity Project, became known as "the father of the hydrogen bomb"—and his interest in furthering the technology would eventually bring about his alienation from most of the scientific community (see chapter 7).

than physical practice), especially nuclear physics, which he felt was the newest, most exciting field of research. In Teller, Mayer found the ideal mentor. He had one of the greatest minds in physics, he loved to talk, and he loved teaching. He was patient, humorous, and almost endlessly creative.

FROM LECTURES TO WRITING

When Maria became pregnant in 1937, she decided against further teaching. She felt too big and too clumsy to stand in front of a class and lecture. She decided to write a textbook with Joe on statistical mechanics, the branch of physics concerning the laws that govern the assemblies of molecules. They thought it would be a short-term project, but it took two years to complete. Their routine went like this: one would write a chapter, the other would edit it, then the first author would rewrite, until they had a chapter that satisfied both scientists. Then they moved on to the next chapter.

They were still working on the book, and Maria was still pregnant, when Joe was suddenly encouraged to leave his position at Johns Hopkins by its new president, Isaiah Bowman. The Depression had nearly wiped out the university's endowment, and government funds for research were severely cut. Bowman thought that forcing out expensive senior faculty members such as Joe Mayer would save the university money.

At the same time, an anti-science movement was sweeping the country. Many felt that scientific developments in technology and automation in the 1920s was contributing to unemployment and the growing economic crisis.

Joe was an associate professor, which at most institutions is a tenured rank, protecting its holder from sudden dismissal. Johns Hopkins did not consider associate professors as tenured. Still, Joe had been there for seven years, and the American Association of University Professors (AAUP) was pushing for the right to automatic tenure after such a length of time. Joe considered allowing the AAUP to fight his case but decided he didn't want to be in the spotlight. Besides, he had two job offers almost immediately: one from the University of Chicago and the other from Columbia.

Joe's dismissal from Johns Hopkins devastated Maria. She also blamed herself for a general sense of chaos in the physics department. She wondered if the space she'd always taken there had been at the expense of someone else who might have made a difference. Maria also wondered whether her German heritage had anything to do with Joe's departure from Johns Hopkins—for with World War II drawing near, an anti-German sentiment was spreading quickly on campus. She found the whole affair heartbreaking.

Joe wasn't nearly as discouraged as his wife by the events. Johns Hopkins gave him two years before the dismissal was to take place, but he resigned on the spot and took the Columbia job for twice the salary he'd earned at Johns Hopkins.

Peter Mayer was born in 1938, just a few months before the family left to go north to Columbia, where Joe would become an associate professor in chemistry.

Maria's situation was even worse than it had been in Baltimore. In fact, she could not claim any academic affiliation to print under her name on the front page of *Statistical Mechanics*, the book that she had co-authored with Joe. Harold Urey brought up the dilemma at a departmental meeting: couldn't some sort of honorary appointment be made, if only for the sake of the book? His request was denied, so Urey assigned Maria to give some chemistry lectures that semester. Printed under her name on the front page of the book was "Lecturer in Chemistry, Columbia University." This was hardly the kind of title that represented her contribution to the book, but it was all that could be legally printed.

The book eventually became a classic in physics curriculums throughout the country. Most people mistakenly believed it had been written entirely by Joe, which helped make his professional reputation. It did little or nothing for Maria, who was thought to be some sort of editorial assistant for the book.

5

Building the Bomb: 1939–1945

I don't like it, and I'm sorry I ever had anything to do with it.
—Physicist Erwin Schrödinger, on quantum mechanics

In 1939, only months before the Mayers left for Columbia, two European scientists arrived in Washington, D.C. to address a conference on theoretical physics. One was Niels Bohr; the other was a young Italian named Enrico Fermi, who had just been awarded the Nobel Prize for his research on radioactivity. Bohr and Fermi brought news to the United States that was both exciting and frightening.

They told a story about two German investigators—Otto Hahn and Fritz Strassman—who had discovered what appeared to be nuclear fission. By bombarding uranium atoms with the nuclear particle called a neutron, the nucleus of the uranium atom could be made to split, releasing a great amount of energy. The investigators theorized that if the fission process

The remains of the Museum of Science and Technology stand at ground zero in Hiroshima, Japan. After the bomb was exploded at Hiroshima, Mayer no longer had a job with the "Substitute Alloy Materials" project, the code name for the research project on creating fissionable U-235. No longer needed, she found herself inexplicably shunned by some of her peers. She returned to part-time teaching at Sarah Lawrence, where at least some of her students respected her.

released secondary neutrons that could be used to split further uranium nuclei, this would free even more neutrons. This would likely generate tremendous amounts of energy.

While there might be some peaceful use for the process, the investigators thought that a weapon of terrible power could be made using nuclear fission. Bohr told the audience

er og Nuttall's Apparat

Along with Enrico Fermi, European physicist Niels Bohr, shown here, was one of the first scientists to bring news about the discovery of nuclear fission to the United States in 1939. Bohr's concerns about the potential use of fission as a powerful weapon were validated only a few years later, when the United States used the "A-bomb" against Japan.

that he was troubled by both the threat of war in Europe and the possibility that nuclear fission could play a part in determining its outcome.

Fermi and his family found a house in Leonia, New Jersey, not far from Columbia, where he had an appointment. The

Mayers also found a house in Leonia, and Maria became good friends with Laura Fermi. Maria took Laura under her wing and showed her some of the more mysterious aspects of American life, such as dropping off clothes at a dry cleaning store and shopping at a supermarket. Laura Fermi had never seen such things before and she was terrified by them at first.

While Maria was helping Laura adjust to life in America, Enrico Fermi was busy trying to persuade the United States government to begin research into what later became known among scientists as "the uranium problem." By 1941, Fermi landed a small grant for experiments to determine whether a self-sustaining chain reaction in nuclear material was practical. Maria worked with him informally, but under a formal oath of secrecy. In December of that year, when the Japanese attacked Pearl Harbor, the drive to create a nuclear fission bomb began in earnest, a project that would eventually involve most of the top scientists in the country but that would cause the Mayers special conflicts.

Fermi left Columbia the following spring for the University of Chicago, where he hoped to build the world's first nuclear reactor. Reactors can be designed to give birth to plutonium, the explosive component of fission bombs. It was the first important development in the production of the atomic bomb.

At Columbia University, where Joe had been appointed to an associate professorship in chemistry, Maria's teaching position started out even shakier than the one at Johns Hopkins. While she had carved out a humble niche for herself at Johns Hopkins, Maria was practically invisible at Columbia.

The prevailing favoritism in academia at the time made it virtually impossible for husband and wife to find employment at the same university. Still, with so many scientists out of work during the 1930s, the Mayers were grateful that at least one of them had found work.

I.I. Rabi, a talented nuclear physicist who was at the school during the 1930s and who considered women unsuited to science because of their temperament, best expressed the atmosphere at Columbia. Rabi believed that a woman's nervous system "makes it impossible for [her] to stay with the thing. Women may go off into science, and they will do well enough, but they will never do great science." (Gabor, 128)

The chairman of the physics department, George Pegram, didn't want Maria anywhere near his territory. When someone arranged for her to use an office in the department, Pegram had her evicted. Finally Harold Urey found a place for her in the chemistry department. He persuaded the higher-ups to let her give a few lectures, if only because the book she'd co-authored with Joe was about to be released. Having "Lecturer in Chemistry" under her name on the title page would lend some credibility to her level of contribution.

Their arrival at Columbia marked the beginning of a close relationship between the Mayers and Harold Urey, a relationship that was to continue throughout Maria's life, as they always seemed to turn up in the same places in later years.

TEACHING AT SARAH LAWRENCE COLLEGE

The Japanese surprise bombing of Pearl Harbor on December 7, 1941, marked the end of Maria's quiet suburban lifestyle. One day later, she accepted a part-time teaching job at nearby Sarah Lawrence College. The offer came out of nowhere. She was given a week to prepare for a meeting with the college's deans to explain how she would go about teaching.

When Maria arrived at the meeting, she told the deans they should consider putting together a course that unified the sciences of astronomy, chemistry, and physics. She admitted to them that it might be more than she could do.

To her surprise, the deans told Maria to proceed. She was hired for her first real teaching job in the United States. She would teach mathematics and the unified science course of her own design and be paid about $1,500 a year for a two-day teaching schedule.

Within days of being hired, Maria was teaching the unified science course to a roomful of girls. Not since her high school days had she been in a classroom filled only with girls. Most of them were busy knitting instead of listening. Some of the girls wondered just what class they were in, and asked what they were supposed to be doing—physics or chemistry. "It's science," she told them. (Dash, *Life*, 291)

No sooner had Maria begun teaching in the spring semester than Joe Mayer landed a job testing conventional weapons at the Aberdeen Proving Grounds in Maryland. The job would keep him away from home five days a week for several years. At the time, it would have been unthinkable for a scientist to turn down work related to the war effort. Joe also spent most Saturdays working at Columbia. Sundays were reserved for family.

Before she had a chance to adjust to teaching at Sarah Lawrence, Maria received a second job offer later that spring. Urey was assembling a secret research group at Columbia to separate uranium-235 (U-235) from the much more abundant uranium-238 (U-238). U-235 was readily fissionable, making it suitable for a bomb; U-238 was not.

A year or so later, the group became part of the Substitute Alloy Materials (SAM) project, which was one of the major research sections of the Manhattan Project, the name given to the development of the atomic bomb. It was charged with the task of mass-producing uranium for use in atomic weapons. Urey was its director of research and because the actual work was for the government, not Columbia University, he was free to hire and pay Maria.

While the job offer was exciting, Maria had serious reservations about accepting. She was being asked to work full-time while Joe was away in Maryland for days at a time. Depriving her children of both parents seemed wrong to Maria. She had been reluctant to take the job at Sarah Lawrence because it meant leaving the children for long periods of time.

Peter was an infant prone to successive colds and other minor ailments. There would be no way to get home quickly if one of the children became sick.

She couldn't turn down Urey, though. Being wanted as a scientist in her own right, not because of her association with Joe Mayer, was flattering to Maria. Finally, she accepted the offer, but she specified that it would be a part-time job and she would never work on Saturdays, even though most of the other scientists worked on the weekend. Further, if either of the children became sick, she would stay home.

Urey, who had always respected Maria as a person as well as a scientist, agreed to those terms. He assigned her to side issues rather than the main line of research in the laboratory. One of her investigations focused on the possibility of separating isotopes (types of atoms of the same element that have different numbers of neutrons in their nuclei) by photochemical reactions. It was nice, clean physics that did not help in the actual separation of isotopes.

Marianne remembered the day her mother announced she would be gone every day during the week and that the children would be cared for by a nursemaid because "she would be happier when she was home if she worked more, and we'd be better off." (Dash, *Life*, 293)

Maria took temporary leave from Sarah Lawrence and hired Alice Kimball, a well-educated English girl who had been stranded in the United States by World War II, to work as a nanny. Neither Marianne nor Peter liked their nanny. They were used to the kindly, affectionate, undereducated German maids and to their mother, who was extremely permissive. The children felt Alice was severe, unsympathetic, and bossy, but they never complained to their mother. They knew she was helping to win the war, a war being fought not against Germany or the German people but against Adolf Hitler. It was a point that was emphasized to the children over and over again, and they repeated it to their friends.

Maria met Nobel Prize–winner Harold Urey at Columbia University. When Urey convinced the university to give Maria a job as a lecturer in chemistry, he opened the door to better academic opportunities for Maria, and the two became great friends. Later, when Urey was put in charge of assembling a secret team of scientists to work on SAM, he invited her to join him in what was an important part of the Manhattan Project.

Some of the neighborhood children were skeptical about these finer points of the war. They felt the war was against all Germans and Maria Goeppert Mayer spoke with a German accent. That made Peter an easy target, because he was awkward and easy to tease.

Maria's careful explanations about whom the war was being fought against could not expose what was in her heart. Her mother had died a few years earlier, but a large extended family of aunts, uncles, and cousins remained in Germany. She feared for their safety during D-Day and the Allied invasion of

Europe. Each day, Maria kept track of the advancing armies by marking their progress on a large wall map. Every pin she placed on the map marked a familiar town or river.

Even more troubling than the armies was the bomb her fellow scientists were working on, a bomb that even she had played a role in creating. It threatened people and a country she loved. She could only pray that the war would be over before the bomb was ready.

A SCIENTIST IN HER OWN RIGHT

While Maria was uncomfortable with her contribution to the weapon, she loved being taken seriously as a scientist for the first time. She worked hard, was utterly conscientious, and found she loved having responsibility. She had been deprived until then of the spoils of hard work—money, recognition, and approval. Before, only Joe and a few colleagues had acknowledged her abilities. Now, she was considered an important piece of a bigger puzzle. Maria had evolved from a fringe-benefit faculty wife into a true professional.

"Here I was suddenly taken seriously [and] considered a good scientist," she said. (Dash, *Life*, 294)

As she had in Baltimore, Maria built an intimate relationship with a handful of colleagues. Some of them would become important to her as the war progressed. In addition to Fermi, she became closer to Edward Teller, who worked at Columbia in 1941 and returned frequently after his departure for Los Alamos in 1942. By the end of the war, Maria was taking her orders directly from Teller and heading up the Opacity Project, which involved studying the thermodynamic properties of matter and radiation at extremely high temperatures, such as during a nuclear explosion.

To get the secret Opacity Project started, Maria had to undergo a security briefing in Washington, D.C. The security officer explained to her that by giving away seemingly unimportant bits of information, someone might disclose more than intended. For example, he said, she didn't need to conceal that there was a new factory at Hanford or that there was work going on at the Metallurgical Laboratory at Chicago. What had to be kept secret was the connection between the two.

Learning that there was secret work going on at the Hanford site in Washington completely surprised Maria. As they left the meeting, Maria told Teller she hoped he would never commit a breach of security as the officer had just done.

In February of 1945, Joe was sent to the Pacific for several months to see how the men trained at Aberdeen were using their weapons. Maria decided she would visit Los Alamos while he was gone. That meant leaving the children in Leonia with the nanny. Laura Fermi and her children had been living in Los Alamos since the summer of 1944. Like most of the wives of scientists working there, Laura had no idea about the project.

With the Mayers it was the other way around. Maria knew what was going on. It was Joe who had to speculate. He knew the work at SAM had somehow been connected to the development of a weapon based on uranium fission. Every scientist in America knew that. In fact, Joe had been asked to work on this secret weapon very early in its development. He'd refused because he couldn't take it seriously.

Joe was convinced an atomic weapon could not be developed in less than 20 or 30 years. He said to Maria when the subject came up, "I'm working on this war; you're working on the next." (Dash, *Life*, 296)

Maria spent close to four years separated from Joe, except for some weekends. The absence weighed heavily on her. Her passion for research, which began during the war years, grew out of her sense of duty to her new country, and out of her increasing loneliness, which was highlighted by the pain and shame of being a German living in the United States. The war became a major burden for Maria. It occupied her thoughts every day. She loved her native country, but she felt it necessary that the Allies develop the bomb first.

Edward Teller, Maria Mayer, Joe Mayer, and James Franck. While at the University of Chicago, Maria worked closely with Teller on his work involving the origin of the elements. This research would spark Maria's interest in finding out why some elements are more stable than others.

Maria found it increasingly difficult to keep the nature of her work a secret. Unlike most of the other German scientists who worked on the bomb, she had left her mother country voluntarily. She loved Germany and the German people and hoped that Hitler, whom she considered an aberration, would be defeated with as little destruction as possible. Other German scientists were not as sure about their country. Some of them felt Hitler was not unique, that he had found thousands of sympathizers to carry out his evil work. Maria also feared that the Germans were working on a similar project and were, in fact, close to success.

When the United States declared victory in Europe on May 8, 1945, Maria was alone in Leonia. Joe was still in the Pacific. A big party was scheduled for all the scientists at Columbia. For Maria, the victory was bittersweet. She could have celebrated peace, but victory for the U.S. implied rejoicing in the defeat of people she loved, people who had suffered while she was safe. Maria decided to stay at home with the children that day.

With Germany no longer an enemy to use the bomb against, pressure mounted for a test. The Japanese were still a threat. It was becoming clear that the bomb had to be finished soon to avoid a bloody land invasion of Japan, which would cost hundreds of thousands of American lives. While Maria was in Los Alamos shortly after V.E. Day, testing the bomb seemed to be all the scientists there could talk about. It was the culmination of all their hard work and passionate dedication.

At first, Maria thought she would stay at Los Alamos for the first test of the bomb at Alamogordo in mid-July. She planned to meet Joe in Albuquerque on his way home from the Pacific so they could travel back East together. Then Maria realized it would be better if she left for Leonia at the end of June. Meeting Joe in New Mexico and not being able to tell him the secret she had been hiding for three years would be too much.

Joe came home earlier than expected, so they did meet in Albuquerque and immediately returned to New Jersey together. A few days later, Maria ran into Urey at Columbia. He had been trying to reach someone at Los Alamos by phone but couldn't connect with anyone. He wondered what it meant. He and Maria were the only people at Columbia who knew the first bomb test was scheduled for mid-July. The significance of the day was clear: the Atomic Age had begun.

The bomb had been tested, and two weeks later it was used to destroy the Japanese city of Hiroshima.

DROPPING THE BOMB

The first atomic bomb was christened "Little Boy." It was loaded onto the battle cruiser USS *Indianapolis* in San Francisco Bay and carried from there to Tinian, an island in the Pacific Ocean.

"Little Boy" was then placed on the *Enola Gay* for the air trip to Japan on August 7, 1945. Paul Tibbets, who piloted the mission, named the plane after his mother, Enola Gay Tibbets.

The crew was nervous during the flight from Tinian to Japan; they were fully aware that they were about to make history. They drank coffee and ate ham sandwiches on the approach to Hiroshima.

Suddenly, the bomb-bay doors opened, and "Little Boy" floated silently toward the ground. The release of the bomb lightened the *Enola Gay* by four tons, and the plane jumped a bit; it then turned homeward.

Tibbets recalled, "A bright light filled the plane. The first shock wave hit us. We were eleven and a half miles . . . from the atomic explosion but the whole airplane cracked and crinkled from the blast. . . . [One of the crew] said he could taste atomic fission. He said it tasted like lead."

Later, scientists would learn that the temperature at the explosion site in Hiroshima reached 5,400 degrees Fahrenheit. Thousands of people were incinerated immediately, and many others died from radiation poisoning in the long fallout period. The total number of deaths as a result of the bombing has been estimated at 140,000.

Two days later, the United States dropped a second atomic bomb, this one on the Japanese city of Nagasaki. The results were similarly devastating: nearly 150,000 people were killed or injured. The bombs effectively ended the Japanese participation in World War II.

Suddenly, peace was upon them. The SAM job no longer existed. Maria returned to her half-time teaching job at Sarah Lawrence.

THE SAM PROJECT ENDS;
MARIA MAYER RETURNS TO OBSCURITY

Despite her important contributions to the SAM project, Maria was still not fully accepted into the academic community. One incident seemed to sum up her relationship with other scientists. Before the war, she and Joe and some friends drove in from Leonia for the weekly early-evening seminars held by the Columbia chemistry department. After the seminar, they went as a group for dinner.

After Joe moved to Aberdeen, Maria attended the seminars and dinners alone. One day, a person from the chemistry department called and told Maria that she was welcome to attend the seminar but that her presence at the dinner—for some unexplained reason—had suddenly become awkward. Maria was so deeply hurt that she never attended another seminar or dinner. She refused to allow Joe to complain about the treatment, as he wanted to do.

Columbia students, most of whom were male, also had a difficult time accepting Maria as a teacher. Several students in her physical chemistry course complained about her methods, especially her rigid grading practices. They were unhappy that she marked their answers wrong even if only one or two numbers were wrong. She never gave partial credit.

"She was a tough taskmaster," said a student. "She was a perfectionist." (Gabor, 132)

While she was angering some Columbia students, Maria was becoming a well-liked teacher at Sarah Lawrence. She was even able to recruit one of her students, Susan Herrick Chandler, to work on the SAM project after her graduation.

To teach the students at Sarah Lawrence, most of whom had no serious background in science, Maria tested her lectures

Sarah Lawrence College in the winter. Maria first began teaching at Sarah Lawrence College in 1942. Though the job was only part-time, it was her first opportunity to earn a respectable salary as an instructor. Teaching a course she designed herself that combined physics, chemistry, and astronomy, she interrupted her work there when she accepted the job at SAM, returning to the university after the A-bomb ended the war in Japan.

on 10-year-old Marianne. If her daughter understood nothing, Maria knew the material was too difficult. If she understood everything, it was too easy.

During the early 1940s, Maria began to lose touch with her children. Between the pressures of her job, the anxiety over the war, and her increasing dedication to science and research, she just couldn't find time to spend with Marianne and Peter. Throughout the war, Maria had a nagging feeling that she was neglecting them. Her feelings were considerably reinforced by Peter's poor performance in school. He had trouble with the

English language, especially with learning to read. Marianne had gone to nursery school speaking only German and had learned English in no time, but Peter seemed to learn nothing. Maria hoped that, with more time now, reading to him would make a difference.

The separation from her parents during the war also affected Marianne. Joe had been gone so much of the time that she felt out of touch with him. Naturally reserved, she couldn't make demands of his attention now that he was home again. "Two scientists in the family is 1.5 too many," she once said. (Gabor, 133)

Although at 12 Marianne was shy, quiet, and well-behaved, she did make one attempt at putting family affairs on a more intimate footing. She told her mother one day that she was sick of hearing talk about science all the time. Maria made a household rule on the spot: no "shop talk" during the cocktail hour or at dinner. It was a rule she was determined to observe from then on.

6

Toward the Magic Numbers: 1945–1948

We have a habit in writing articles published in scientific journals to make the work as finished as possible, to cover up all the tracks, to not worry about the blind alleys or describe how you had the wrong idea first, and so on. So there isn't any place to publish, in a dignified manner, what you actually did in order to get to do the work.
—Richard P. Feynman, Nobel Lecture, 1966

Both the man of science and the man of action live always at the edge of mystery, surrounded by it.
—J. Robert Oppenheimer, at Columbia University, 1945

In mid-July of 1945, only a few days after the secret tests at Alamogordo, three representatives of the University of Chicago traveled to a hilltop home in Santa Fe, near Los Alamos, where they ate lunch and discussed with Fermi and a few colleagues

A group photo at the University of Chicago of scientists who helped to develop the atomic bomb. Seated, second from the left, is Harold Urey, and Enrico Fermi is second from the right. Edward Teller is standing at the far left; Joe Mayer is fourth from the right, almost in the center.

plans to set up a group of basic research institutes at the University of Chicago. The institutes would be a meeting ground for science and industry and staffed by physicists, chemists, biologists, and engineers brought together by a desire to resume their scientific careers and return to unclassified research and university teaching.

Shortly after the war ended, Teller, Urey, and Joe Mayer all were offered jobs at Chicago. Urey was the first to accept. Joe was offered a full professorship in the Institute for Nuclear Studies, but he and Maria wanted to visit the university and the city where they would live before he accepted.

When Joe told the Chicago people he was ready to accept, they turned to Maria. They said they had been thinking about making an offer to her for a long time, but they knew she would never move to Chicago without Joe. Now that he was coming, it made sense for her to work there, too.

They offered Maria an assistant professorship and membership in the Institute for Nuclear Studies. There was no salary, not even a token stipend, because of the university's strictly observed nepotism clause, which prevented the hiring of husband and wife even if they worked in different departments. Still, she would have her own office and she would be allowed to fully participate in all university activities.

The nepotism policy really didn't bother Maria. The people responsible for the rule were distant and unreachable. The people she worked with every day respected and valued her work. She was happy to be reunited with friends and colleagues. She looked forward to working in an atmosphere charged with potential for the new ideas in basic research that had emerged during the course of her war work.

Even without a salary, Maria took to her research with new excitement. The University of Chicago was "the first place where I was not considered a nuisance, but greeted with open arms," she said. (Dash, *Triumph*, 20) She must have found it satisfying when, after she and her husband both were invited to the University of California in 1959, Chicago quickly forgot its rigid nepotism rule. They offered Maria, then in her 50s, a salary to stay. It had taken more than 20 years to persuade someone to pay her for her work in the academic world.

This time, the Mayers would live in the city, not in the suburbs as they had in Leonia. Maria had never liked the suburbs. "The women all talked about their babies, and the men talked science," she said. (Dash, *Triumph*, 20)

On Chicago's South Side they found a big old house with five bedrooms, six fireplaces, a third floor that had once been a ballroom, and space outdoors for several gardens. Maria fell in love with the place. They bought it and never regretted the decision. In time, Joe built a greenhouse upstairs, on a balcony attached to the ballroom. Maria grew orchids there. It was one of the many pleasures that awaited them in Chicago.

Peter flourished in Chicago. He refused to attend the University's private school. Instead, he went to public school, where his reading difficulties gradually disappeared. He was bright, maybe even remarkably bright, although still tall, skinny, and as awkward as ever.

Peter and Marianne fought continuously, or so Maria thought. She couldn't intervene because she had no way of dealing with the anger and jealousy the children were expressing. Joe was no help, either. He never seemed to be interested in the children or their problems at the time, perhaps because he had been away from them for so long.

Likewise, the war years had taken their toll on the Mayers' marriage. Even though they had gotten back together, much of their old intimacy was gone. Maria drank heavily and smoked even more. She was no longer the young beauty of Goettingen. Rumors circulated around the university campus that Joe had his eye on other women. Eventually, Maria confided to her son that she and his father were not getting along.

When Max Born's son visited Maria in Chicago in the late 1950s, he barely recognized her. She had gained much weight and smoked heavily; Gustav Born's impression was that she was not happy. The Mayers had begun to discuss divorce.

A portrait of Mayer after she joined the faculty of the University of California at La Jolla. She missed her home in Chicago, and the move proved difficult for her, but Mayer was overjoyed to finally receive her due as a full professor of physics at the age of 53. Not long after the move, however, she suffered a debilitating stroke.

DISCOVERING "MAGIC NUMBERS"

Maria had come to Chicago determined to continue her work on the Opacity Project with Edward Teller. Like the Mayers, Teller had accepted an appointment at the University of Chicago, and the Opacity Project was housed in the university's Metallurgical Laboratory, where the initial work on the nuclear chain reaction had been carried out during the war.

The Metallurgical Laboratory went out of existence to make way for the Argonne National Laboratory on July 1, 1946, under the newly formed Atomic Energy Commission. Maria accepted a regular appointment as senior physicist in the Theoretical Physics Division. The main interest at Argonne was nuclear physics, a field in which she had had little experience, and so she gladly accepted the opportunity to learn what she could about the subject. She continued to hold this part-time appointment throughout her years in Chicago, while maintaining her voluntary appointment at the University.

Teller wanted someone to work with him on a fascinating theory about the origin of the elements. He wanted a fellow scientist to serve as an audience and a sounding board for ideas. Teller also wanted someone to do the involved mathematics, one of Maria's areas of expertise. She welcomed the idea— which would eventually lead to her Nobel Prize–winning work on the shell structure of the nucleus. Working with Teller had always been instructive and exciting.

Teller's theory was in line with current thinking at the time, that most elements had been formed when the universe was very young, perhaps as part of its creation process. The theory was later abandoned.

Teller wrote: "Our theory continues to appear to me as something amusing, but unfortunately, neither she nor I believe it any more. It is now believed that the elements have been mostly formed in supernova explosions and have been accumulating through the ages." (Dash, *Life*, 310)

Soon, both Maria and Teller began to notice that a few elements—tin and lead are good examples—were much more abundant than their theory, or any other theory, could explain. They wondered how this could happen and visited each other to share ideas. For an element to be extremely abundant means that it has a stable nucleus, for unstable elements are subject to radioactive decay and lose or gain electrons to form new chemical combinations. In essence, they change into different elements. Maria and Teller wondered why those particular nuclei, the lead and the tin and others, were so remarkably stable.

As usual, Teller was involved in a number of projects at

THE SCANDAL THAT SPLIT PHYSICS

J. Robert Oppenheimer was one of the principal minds behind the development of the atomic bomb—if not *the* principal mind. He served as director of the Manhattan Project, the first testing of atomic technology, and he came to regret his involvement afterward. Edward Teller participated in the Manhattan Project; when funding was pulled from the atomic program after the tragedy of Hiroshima, Teller, dissatisfied, set up his own lab and sought a more powerful explosive: the hydrogen bomb.

The Soviet Union, the United States' major enemy at the time, tested a crude kind of hydrogen bomb in 1949, causing the U.S. to restore funding to the atomic project, this time with Teller heading the research effort. The first American hydrogen bomb was tested in 1952.

The atmosphere in the country then was one of suspicion; Senator Joseph McCarthy, as head of the House Un-American Activities Committee, was conducting hearings to determine whether legions of accused people actually sympathized with the Communist Party. Fearing that Oppenheimer would the same time. One day when he was out of town, Maria had time to ponder the situation. She gathered the information about elements and nuclei that they had been studying and painstakingly inspected it.

When Teller was around, she didn't say much. He was quick and dazzling with his thoughts. She felt like an apprentice. Being alone seemed to work in Maria's favor. Suddenly, she discovered that "in all these nuclei either the number of protons or the number of neutrons was very special." (Gabor, 142) Eventually, Maria discovered a host of "special numbers" in the nuclei of elements, which she came to refer to as "magic numbers." Maria liked the phrase

jeopardize the hydrogen bomb project, the Atomic Energy Commission, successor to the Manhattan Project, revoked his security clearance. A hearing was held soon afterward, at which many of Oppenheimer's colleagues testified on his behalf in the hope of seeing his clearance restored. Teller testified *against* Oppenheimer: "I thoroughly disagreed with him in numerous issues, and his actions frankly appeared to me confused and complicated. To this extent I feel that I would like to see the vital interests of this country in hands which I understand better, and therefore trust more."

The decision of the House Un-American Activities Committee, the body overseeing the hearings, was that clearance should not be restored; Oppenheimer's career was ruined, and the scientific community blamed Teller for it. Many of Teller's former colleagues now ostracized him, and Teller, badly shaken by the reaction, went into a kind of seclusion. Nevertheless, he and Mayer corresponded from 1939 until the end of her life.

because she thought it captured the spirit of mystery attached to the numbers.

Maria discovered that the most stable nuclei have any one of a few magic numbers—that is, they have 2, 8, 20, 28, 50, 82, or 126 neutrons or protons. Although other scientists had discovered some of the magic numbers earlier, their existence was not considered important to nuclear structure. Maria, who was not aware of the earlier discoveries, added new ones to the known list. As the numbers increased, the mystery deepened.

When Teller returned from his trip, Maria tried to interest him in her discovery, but he was more focused on the development of nuclear weapons and the origin of elements. He wasn't interested in magic numbers. Maria began collecting more information on nuclei from nuclear experiments at the University of Chicago. Over and over again, the data proved to be producing the very same numbers, pointing to a nuclear symmetry similar to that of an atom, where electrons orbit the nucleus.

The magic numbers indicated the potential for great stability within the nucleus, much like the structure of certain atoms that contain nuclei with such tightly bound electrons that they do not combine easily with other chemical compounds by losing or gaining an electron. The existence of nuclei with tightly bound "shells" of neutrons and protons that prevent them from breaking down into other elements could help explain why some elements are much more abundant in nature than others.

Maria would return home at night excited about the research she had done during the day. Instead of sitting down and listening to what the children had done all day, she would fill the air with cigarette smoke and talk nonstop about the magic numbers. Joe would nod and tell her to keep accumulating data—though theorists were more comfortable with explanations than facts.

The mystery occupied Maria's mind day and night. "I never got rid of thinking, what are they?" she said. "They lived with me for a year." (Dash, *Triumph*, 24)

7

Spin-Orbit Coupling Becomes Clear: 1948–1963

Every great and deep difficulty bears in itself its own solution.
It forces us to change our thinking in order to find it.
—Niels Bohr

Your theory is crazy, but it's not crazy enough to be true.
—Niels Bohr to a young physicist

Mayer also began visiting Fermi, the only physicist in Chicago who seemed interested in her work, and while speaking with him one afternoon she hit on the final piece of the magic-numbers puzzle. They were in her office when Fermi was called to take a long-distance telephone call. As he reached the door, he turned to ask a question about spin-orbit coupling.

In a sudden flash of insight, Maria was able to explain why certain magic numbers fit inside certain nuclei. She knew right away that she had solved the mystery. It was an

The renowned physicist Enrico Fermi was one of Mayer's mentors and helped inspire her to form her theories about magic numbers and shell structure in atoms. Typical of her shy demeanor, she at first tried to publish her paper on the subject as a co-author with Fermi, but Fermi insisted that she would receive her rightful credit only by publishing the work under her name alone.

awesome sensation that she was never quite able to describe, one that was so forceful that it wiped everything else from her mind at that moment. Even as Fermi was walking out the door, Mayer was reaching for paper and a pencil to begin the calculations that would prove what she knew was correct.

Fermi returned about ten minutes later, and Mayer started to explain her new theory. Her words came out quickly, and not to Fermi's satisfaction; he preferred a slower, more detailed, more methodical explanation. According to Joe, Fermi's response was restrained: "Tomorrow, when you are less excited, you can explain it to me," he said with a smile as he left the office. (Gabor, 144)

What Maria had figured out was that the value of the magic number inside each stable nucleus was a function of two interrelated quantities: the spin and orbital angular momentum of each particle. Each nucleon spins around its own axis. At the same time, it has a momentum within an orbit.

Scientists knew that nucleons had both spin and orbital angular momentum. It was Maria who figured out that the relationship between the two had a significant effect on the energy level of each nucleon and therefore determined whether it contained magic numbers, and the value of those numbers. The reason no one had thought to connect the two forces was that in the atomic model, the spin of the electron has very little interaction with its orbital angular momentum.

Spin-orbit coupling is like a roomful of people dancing a waltz. The couples rotate, each dancer revolving around a point between herself and her partner, as they progress around the room in a circle. Each smaller, twirling couple-circle is a part of the larger revolution. (Another possible analogy would be to a "teacup" ride at an amusement park.) If some of the couples circle the room clockwise while the others move counterclockwise, then twice as many dancers can fit into the circle, or shell. Furthermore, some of the couples progressing counterclockwise can rotate clockwise, and vice versa. Nuclear particles behave similarly, but there is an important difference in the energy required for a particle to twirl one way as opposed to the other. As Mayer put it: "Anyone who has ever danced the fast waltz knows

that it's easier to spin one way around than the other."
(Dash, *Triumph*, 26)

Inspired by the new perspective, she recognized it as the explanation for magic numbers as well as proof of the shell theory of the nucleus. With spin-orbit coupling, the number of possible paths along which nuclear particles could travel increased. Wherever a shell was most tightly bound in place, there were the magic numbers.

The magic numbers, then, can be thought of as representing the number of dancers who form a completed circle, with just enough room in the circle for them. The circle resists being broken by any extra dancer passing by. In effect, the number of dancers represents the number of nuclear particles in a shell.

In April of 1948, Maria wrote up some of her preliminary findings. Although she had written important papers before, this was perhaps the first time that Maria experienced the physical and emotional excitement that accompanies a profound leap of creative insight. Still, she was afraid to present her ideas to the scientific community because she feared they were not as original as she thought. She had read papers dealing with magic numbers that had been written by two other scientists, Lothar Nordheim and Eugene Feenberg. Maria was concerned that they may have influenced her thinking, even though they had drawn conclusions very different from hers.

Instead of compiling a detailed explanation of her theory, Maria wrote a short "letter to the editor" that was published, together with short statements by Nordheim and Feenberg, in the June 1949 issue of the magazine *Physical Review*.

During the next few months, Joe prodded Maria several times to write up her theory in proper form and length, with all the supporting data, for publication. He didn't understand her reluctance. Neither could Teller, who was no longer a partner in her work but remained interested in whatever interested Maria.

Maria was very different from her husband and Teller. She was modest, lacked aggressiveness, hated arguments and competition, and saw no value in beating someone else out. As a working scientist, she was used to being just barely tolerated. Neither her personality nor her experience encouraged her to speak up. One day, Joe forced a pencil into Maria's hand and ordered her to begin writing. Finally, in December of 1949, Maria published two lengthy papers on her discovery in *Physical Review*.

Maria also had to be talked out of submitting her papers under a dual byline with Fermi. She wanted to do that to recognize how their conversations had inspired her. Fermi had to convince her that the theory was her own and that to have the name of a more famous scientist attached to the paper would overshadow her own contribution.

MARIA'S "TWIN BROTHER": COLLABORATION WITH HANS JENSEN

As it turned out, Maria almost lost credit for her discovery to another scientist in the highly competitive world of physics research. After the publication of her brief letter explaining the discovery in 1949, the German physicist J. Hans Daniel Jensen rushed into print with his own version of the shell model. It was almost identical to what Maria had presented.

Maria's initial reaction was disappointment at not being the first and only discoverer of the shell model. After further thought, though, she realized that if Jensen had come to the same conclusion independently, then they must be correct.

Instead of being rivals, the two scientists developed a close friendship that would lead to the last major collaboration of Maria's scientific life. She began writing letters to him, often referring to "our theory." In his replies, Jensen wrote of "your theory."

When Mayer and Jensen met in person for the first time in the summer of 1951, they got along immediately. Maria and Joe had traveled to Germany as State Department consultants charged with renewing contacts with German physicists and chemists. Jensen, a respected physicist from the University of Heidelberg, received them warmly and immediately arranged for Maria to receive an invitation to the university for the following summer.

The Mayers returned the favor. In the fall of 1951, Jensen arrived in the United States and traveled around the country as a guest lecturer for several months, always returning to Chicago to stay with the Mayers when he had the opportunity. By February of 1952, Jensen had spent close to two months living with the Mayers.

For Maria, Jensen was more than just a collaborator on scientific research. He was also something of a "soul mate." Widowed for several years, Jensen was a playful eccentric who put things off. He loved gardening but lived alone on the Heidelberg campus in a small apartment that also served as his office.

While there was some speculation that Jensen and Maria Mayer were having an affair, it was more likely that Maria found in Jensen the brother she'd never had. While Joe could be tough and arrogant, Jensen was gentle and friendly. Maria and Jensen shared a love of music, while Joe was tone-deaf. They also found special meaning in the fact that they shared the same birthday and eyeglass prescription. Sometimes they joked about being twins who had been separated at birth. Jensen even took to signing his letters to Maria "with love, your twin brother." (Gabor, 148)

Early in their collaboration, Maria and Jensen agreed to co-author a book entitled *Elementary Theory of Nuclear Shell Structure*, which was published in 1955. Maria spent much of her time coaxing Jensen to get his portion of the book finished.

When it was finally completed, most colleagues assumed Maria had done most of the work, and they were probably correct. During the four years it took to write the book, the Mayer–Jensen shell model came to be accepted throughout the physics community, on both sides of the ocean. The book only confirmed its importance.

Even while she was working with Jensen, Maria was assuming a leadership role at Argonne. She led a small group of graduate students that became the focal point of a shell-model theory group until Maria left the University of Chicago in 1959. Her style changed from a broad interest in many kinds of physics to a single-minded concern with the effects of the shell model.

Although Maria's prominence in the scientific community was creating new opportunities, life in Chicago had begun to lose its appeal. The biggest blow came when Fermi died of cancer in 1954. James Franck, another close friend, suffered a series of heart attacks that reduced his scientific activity until his death in 1964. Edward Teller lost track of his closest friends after the McCarthy scandal of 1954.

A MOVE TO CALIFORNIA AND A FULL PROFESSORSHIP

In 1959, Maria and Joe both received offers of full professorships at the new campus of the University of California at San Diego. They accepted, and planned to live in La Jolla, which was said to be beautiful. It was near the ocean with plenty of gardens. Plus, the Ureys were already there, so they would have friends close by.

The best part of moving to California was that Maria would finally hold a full professorship in physics, with a full salary to match. Within 24 hours of learning about the offer from the University of California, the University of Chicago

Hans Jensen was a co-recipient of the Nobel Prize in Physics with Maria Mayer, with whom he developed the shell model. At first, the two were competitors, but when Mayer realized that Jensen had independently developed the same theory as she had but had not represented her original concepts as his own, the two became friends. Indeed, her and Jensen's personalities were so compatible that Mayer came to love Jensen like the brother she'd never had.

conveniently abandoned its nepotism rule and tried to persuade the Mayers to stay. They didn't change their minds; they knew it was time to leave the Midwest.

Before they could leave for California, though, they had to deal with an important family matter. Marianne, who had refused to become a scientist, had become engaged to Donat Wenzel, an astrophysicist whose father had been a physicist and an old friend of the Mayers. Maria planned a beautiful wedding, then the Mayers faced the difficult task of moving from Chicago to California. No matter how beautiful La Jolla might be, no matter what honors and dignities awaited, dismantling the Chicago household and moving everything was a long, hard job. When they finally reached La Jolla and moved into a roomy, modern house facing the Pacific Ocean, no one seemed to notice just how tired Maria looked.

The move took a toll on Maria's health. In October, shortly after arriving in California, she fell ill. Doctors never determined whether her condition was due to an infection of her nervous system or a stroke, but she lost the feeling in her left arm and found it difficult to speak. She tired easily but never stopped smoking—it was too late to stop, she thought.

By Christmas, Maria was out of the hospital, determined not to allow her illness to affect Joe's life. A year or so after the stroke, Maria dined at the house of a young colleague. After the other guests had left the table, this colleague stood behind her chair, waiting for her to stand, as politeness dictated that he do. When she started to rise, he pulled out the chair—realizing only afterward that she had only been shifting her position on the seat. Maria crashed unceremoniously to the bare wooden floor. As he stooped to help her up, fearful that she might be injured and feeling guilty because it was his fault, he was amazed that her first words to him were, "It's all right—no one saw."

That fall, speculation flew on both sides of the Atlantic

Ocean about who would win that year's Nobel Prize. Maria and Jensen were mentioned frequently for their shell-model theory. On November 3, 1963, Maria and Joe were awakened at 2:00 A.M. by a telephone call; Joe said it was for Maria, from Stockholm. She in turn found this strange, for she didn't know anyone who lived in Stockholm—but Joe had already run downstairs to chill a bottle of champagne.

The caller was a Swedish reporter announcing that Maria and Jensen had been awarded the Nobel Prize. "I really don't know what to say!" Maria cried. "Is it really true? I still can't believe it's true." (Dash, *Life*, 337)

In Heidelberg, Hans Jensen's first reaction was complete disbelief. A decade earlier a German newspaper had mistakenly reported that he had won the Nobel Prize. He thought this was a mistake, too. "I have had previous experience with this kind of nonsense," he said. (Dash, *Life*, 337)

Two hours after receiving the telephone call, when they finally got around to calling Marianne with the good news that Maria had become only the second woman ever to win the Nobel Prize in Physics (Madam Curie being the first), the couple was a more than a little drunk. "I got this call in the middle of the night, and I was sure my mother was tipsy," recalled Marianne. "In the morning I called them back because I was sure I had dreamt the whole thing." (Gabor, 149)

The next day, reporters and camera crews descended on the Mayers' house. A steady stream of telegrams and flowers arrived. For 48 hours, the house was practically under siege. "La Jolla Mother Wins Nobel Prize" was the headline in one newspaper.

At first, Maria seemed strangely subdued for someone who had just won a prestigious award. Some friends felt Joe was more excited than Maria, but she was simply overwhelmed by the number of calls she received from people offering congratulations, some of whom she had not had contact with for years.

ALFRED NOBEL

Alfred B. Nobel (1833–1896) was a Swedish chemist and engineer who invented dynamite. He left $9 million in his will to establish the Nobel Prizes, which are awarded annually in six areas (peace, literature, physics, chemistry, physiology or medicine, and economics). They are awarded without regard to nationality "to those who, during the preceding year, shall have conferred the greatest benefit on mankind."

It may seem odd that the inventor of a powerful explosive would endow a group of awards that includes a peace prize, but Nobel was an industrialist with a conscience. His invention made the dangerous processes of blasting rock and the construction of canals and tunnels relatively safe.

Nobel also contributed to the inventions of synthetic rubber, artificial silk, and synthetic leather and held more than 350 patents. But his interests were not limited to science: In fact, he was a lover of English literature and poetry and wrote several novels and poems. At his death, he left a library of more than 1,500 books on topics ranging from fiction to philosophy.

Members of Nobel's family were shocked when they learned that he had left his fortune to the establishment of the Nobel Prize program. They contested his will, but his final wishes were executed and the first awards were distributed in 1901, on the fifth anniversary of his death.

The Sveriges Riksbank (Bank of Sweden), established the prize in economics in 1968. Stockholm's Royal Swedish Academy of Sciences administers the awards in physics and chemistry. The Karolinska Institute awards the prize in physiology or medicine, and the Swedish Academy oversees the prize in literature. The Norwegian Nobel Committee, awards the peace prize.

Even in her brightest moment, Maria never received the kind of credit she deserved. Old friends in Germany, asked by the media to comment on Maria's award, remembered her as "the beauty of Goettingen." American friends described her marvelous parties and her lush garden. At a press conference on the lawn of the San Diego campus, a reporter asked Joe whether he thought of the woman beside him as a wife or as a scientist. Startled, he replied, "Why, a wife, of course."

8

Looking Back on a Life in Science

In reading Maria's papers one is struck by the clarity and conciseness of her writing. Her intuition has hardly been matched. She seemed naturally to know the right way to try whatever the problem was. Unlike many theorists, she was very deferential to experimental data and extremely aware of the value of checking theory with experiment. She has, without doubt, set a new watermark in this century for women physicists.
—**From the University of California's *In Memoriam*, 1975**

Late in the afternoon of December 10, 1963, eight men and one woman, all dressed in elegant evening clothes, met in a backstage room at the Concert Hall in Stockholm, Sweden. The King of Sweden and the royal family were gathered in a private parlor nearby.

When the audience of 2,000 had filled the Concert Hall, King, Queen, and royal grandchildren entered to take their

The ceremonies for the Nobel Prize presentation are full of fanfare. The tradition of the awards, which are presented by the King of Sweden, was somewhat overwhelming for the modest Mayer, who felt "very small" as she met the King to receive her prize.

places in the front row. The audience rose before the King entered and sat down only after he sat. When the doors to the backstage room were opened and a fanfare of trumpets announced the appearance onstage of the year's nine Nobel laureates, though, it was the King—tall, aged, hawk-faced, and ghostly thin—who first rose to greet them. It was a sign of respect that became for many the most memorable part of Nobel week.

Nobel laureates were seated to one side of the stage; Nobel Committee members sat on the other side. Maria, dressed in a floor-length green brocade evening gown, found the lights set up for the television cameras almost painfully hot. She couldn't see her husband, who wondered how she would endure several hours without cigarettes and worried over certain details of the ceremony that lay ahead. Maria herself was elated at being the only woman onstage, the only woman with a Nobel Prize in science, and the first woman ever to win it for theoretical science. As excited and apprehensive as she was, Maria wondered why she wasn't more keyed up, why she felt a faint sense of anticlimax to the evening. "To my surprise, winning the prize wasn't half as exciting as doing the work itself," she said. "That was the fun—seeing it work out." (Gabor, 150)

THE NOBEL COMMITTEE ON MAYER'S CONTRIBUTION

It is customary during the Nobel Prize Committee presentation ceremony to summarize the laureates' contributions to their fields. The speech given by a member of the Nobel Committee for Physics at the ceremony in 1963, when Maria Goeppert Mayer and Hans Jensen shared the Prize with Eugene Wigner, details the effect of the shell model on the science of physics:

> A paper published by Goeppert Mayer in 1948 marked the beginning of a new era in the appreciation of the shell model. For the first time convincing evidence was there given for the existence of the higher magic numbers and it was stressed that the experiments support the existence of closed shells very strongly.
>
> Somewhat later Goeppert Mayer . . . published the new idea which was needed for the explanation of the higher magic numbers. The idea was that a nucleon should have different energies when it "spins" in the same or opposite sense as it revolves around the nucleus.
>
> Goeppert Mayer and Jensen collaborated later on the

Still, in the weeks leading up to the ceremony, there were moments that Maria cherished—none more than the day an enormous bouquet of flowers arrived from Max Born, who was filled with pride over his protégé's accomplishment. He also released to the newspapers a glowing account of Maria's life. She couldn't help basking in the glow of Born's affection and approval.

There was also a trip to Scandinavia that turned into one long celebration. Maria and Joe stopped in Denmark and then joined Jensen in Sweden. They were pleasantly surprised to find that the normally disheveled professor had bought an entire

development of the shell model. They published together a book, where they applied the model to the extensive experimental material on atomic nuclei. They gave convincing evidence for the great importance of the shell model in systematizing this material and predicting new phenomena concerning the ground state and the low excited states of the nuclei. The general methods introduced by Wigner have been most important for the applications of the shell model. It has also been possible to give a deeper justification of the shell model. Its fundamental importance has thereby been further confirmed. . . .

Professor Goeppert Mayer, Professor Jensen: Your work on the shell model, which you started independently and then pursued in collaboration, has shed new light on the structure of atomic nuclei. It constitutes a most striking advance in the correlation of nuclear properties. Your work has inspired an ever-increasing number of new investigations and has been indispensable for the later work, both experimental and theoretical, on atomic nuclei.

wardrobe to wear during the week of parties and receptions.

Of the four categories in which Nobel Prizes are awarded in Stockholm—physics, chemistry, physiology or medicine, and literature—physics has always been honored first because it was mentioned first in Alfred Nobel's will. That meant the three physicists—Eugene Wigner, who won half the prize, and Maria Goeppert Mayer and Hans Jensen, who shared the other half—were the first of the nine to be presented. A speech in Swedish by a member of the Swedish Academy of Sciences introduced them as a group, then introduced each of the three individually. First Wigner, then Maria, then Jensen crossed the stage and received the Nobel medal and diploma from the King.

It was this brief but very public performance that troubled Maria Goeppert Mayer in advance. Although she carried it out neatly enough, she was terrified by the thought of coming forward and walking down a step to stand before the King, who towered over her, literally and figuratively.

Mayer held out her right hand to grasp his, and an aide who followed her took the medal and the diploma, for Mayer's left hand and arm were almost completely paralyzed from the stroke she'd suffered three years earlier. Her right hand had little strength and no feeling. She was unable to carry the gold medal, which weighed half a pound, or the diploma, a splendid work of illuminated lettering in a gold-tooled binding of blue leather that was as heavy and awkward as it was handsome.

Still, the ceremony went smoothly. The handshake had seemed successful, and the King had smiled. Mayer backed away from the royal presence, up the step, and onto the stage again. It was a difficult maneuver, made harder by the floor-length dress she wore.

Once Mayer was safely onstage again, standing among the ferns and massed white chrysanthemums and classical statuary, her official responsibilities for the evening were over. She had

Mayer was the second woman to win the Nobel Prize in Physics, the first to win it in theoretical physics, and the first American woman to win it at all. "To my surprise," she said of her Nobel, "winning the prize wasn't half as exciting as doing the work itself. That was the fun— seeing it work out."

only to listen to the speeches, enjoy the symphonic music in between, and try squinting past the bright lights to locate her husband. Had she been able to see him, Maria would have been amazed to note that Joe Mayer had burst into tears while watching his wife take her place near the bust of Alfred Nobel.

Standing on the platform, Maria felt "very small" by comparison to the great scientists who had stood there before her. She thought of her old friend and teacher Max Born, who was now living in retirement in Edinburgh, of Enrico Fermi, and of her father—what would he have said if he were still alive? "He might have felt his advice to me, 'Never become a woman,' had really come true." (Dash, *Life*, 233)

"NEVER BECOME A WOMAN!"

Maria's father had encouraged her to have a profession, not to wait for a man to take care of her, for he had seem the talents of too many women wasted on conventional motherhood. But he'd never thought she would go so far as to win the Nobel Prize. Others were surprised at the win, too; "I always thought Maria was competent," said a physicist who had known her family in the 1940s. "But . . . if you had asked me about her chances of winning a Nobel Prize, my answer probably would have been, 'Are you kidding?'" (Dash, *Life*, 233)

Another physicist said Maria's achievement was all the more remarkable because of her age, the fact that she had only recently come into the field of physics from chemistry, and "most of all because she was a woman."

After the ceremony in Sweden, Maria returned to La Jolla, California, put her Nobel medal in a bank vault, displayed a gold-plated copy in a glass case in her living room, and took up daily life again—teaching, doing research, gardening, traveling, and giving parties. In her sixties, she had the same blue eyes with the same dreamy expression in them that pictures from her Goettingen days revealed. Her hair was tinted auburn, and her complexion was still lovely, but she had grown frail. The stroke had slowed her walk and slightly blurred her speech, so much so that she would never again work with the narrow, focused intensity she'd had before.

For many scientists, the saddest result of such physical disability would have been the loss of the ability to work. Maria accepted her limitations in her own way, by overcoming trouble before self-pity could develop. In the midst of her stroke, with a strange object thrashing in front of her face—she learned later it was her left hand—Maria's only thought was about how difficult it would be for her husband to have an invalid wife. She didn't worry so much about herself as how it would affect Joe.

As for Joe, he hardly changed at all over the years. He was

brisk, energetic, humorous, and always protective of Maria. She understood that everything in her life would have been different without him. Joe was the one who wanted her to work, and who begged to be allowed to fight for her. When the children were young and Maria was tempted to stay at home with them, Joe insisted that with part-time help, the job of running a household, overseeing children, and entertaining on a lavish scale should take no more than a couple of hours a day.

HER FRUSTRATIONS REVEALED

Winning the Nobel Prize couldn't begin to fill the emptiness Maria felt over her illness, her age, and her estrangement from her family. Nor could it compensate for the opportunities that had been denied to her when she was younger and had all her faculties.

The gulf between Maria and her children widened after the move to La Jolla. Marianne lived in Michigan with her husband and rarely visited. Peter, who had received a bachelor's degree in physics from Cal Tech, decided to abandon science to pursue a master's degree in economics, much to Maria's dismay. Peter was so eager to escape from his parents' shadow that he refused to attend the Nobel Prize ceremony, despite their repeated pleas. Marianne, who said she would have been happy to be there, was never invited.

When Maria died of a heart attack in 1972 at the age of 65, eulogies and editorials celebrated her as one of the century's most important physicists. A few months later, at a symposium of the American Physical Society in New York, several colleagues recalled Maria's soft-spoken manner and consistently pleasant disposition. Their memories were of an agreeable, noncompetitive scientist who never allowed her frustrations to end in bitterness, who had never been anything but a lady.

How they remembered Mayer was a problem for some of the female physicists at the symposium. They were upset that the men saw her first as a woman, then as a scientist. "Obviously, they weren't listening," said Fay Azenberg-Selove, a physicist who was struggling for tenure at the University of Pennsylvania at the time. She said Mayer "was extremely angry about the fact that she had not had a full professorship until shortly before winning the Nobel Prize." (Gabor, 152)

Azenberg-Selove met Mayer at a conference in Michigan in 1955. During the cocktail hour, the two women chatted. They didn't know each other well, but since they were among the few females at the conference it just seemed natural that they talk.

Mayer was 49 at the time, but she looked much older. She stood hunched over, absent-mindedly sipping her drink, when Azenberg-Selove told Mayer that she had just become engaged. Almost immediately, Mayer took her younger colleague into a private room, poured her a drink, and began to describe the kind of life she would have. Trying to be a woman with a career in science while married to a scientist would be difficult, Mayer warned her. It would be hard to find a job in the same geographic location as her husband. Academia would have an excuse not to treat her seriously because of her marriage.

Mayer's strong words of warning were surprising because they were so out of character. Generally, she was uncomfortable talking about herself. She'd once been in the habit of confiding some of her innermost thoughts to other women, but she had given that up years before. She had never complained about the discrimination, the nepotism rules, or the frustration and self-doubt she quietly endured.

She had always claimed that she would never have made it as a scientist without her husband. "A woman scientist should never marry anyone but another scientist," she once said. (Gabor, 104) She felt that science was, ultimately, collaboration, and if all else failed, a woman scientist should at least be able to collaborate with her husband.

For Maria Mayer, marriage to a fellow scientist meant that she would always have someone to collaborate with, but it also meant that she was rarely recognized by the academic community for her own intellect and scientific contributions. She overcame discrimination and attempts to relegate her to academic obscurity, though, to become only the second woman in history to win the Nobel Prize in Physics. This is a testimony as much to her persistence as to her brilliance as a scientist.

Chronology

1906   Born on June 28 to Friedrich and Maria Goeppert in Kattowitz, Germany (now Poland).

1921   Leaves public elementary school to enter the Frauenstudium, a three-year private school, to prepare for the entrance examination for Goettingen's Georgia-Augusta University.

1922   Enrico Fermi arrives in Goettingen to study physics with Max Born.

1923   The Frauenstudium closes; Maria passes the entrance examination for Goettingen's Georgia-Augusta University (University of Goettingen).

1924   Enrolls as a student of mathematics at the University of Goettingen.

1927   Joins Max Born's physics seminar at Goettingen; changes her major from mathematics to physics. Friedrich Goeppert dies.

1929   Joe Mayer arrives at Goettingen and rents a room at the Goeppert house.

1930   Maria Goeppert and Joe Mayer are married; Maria completes her Ph.D. thesis; Joe accepts an associate professorship in chemistry at Johns Hopkins University in Baltimore, Maryland; Maria works as a translator of German correspondence.

1933   Daughter Marianne is born is May; Maria becomes a citizen of the U.S.

1937   Maria stops teaching when she becomes pregnant with Peter.

1938   Joe is dismissed from his position at Johns Hopkins but is hired almost immediately at Columbia University at twice the salary; son Peter is born.

1939   Maria lectures on chemistry at Columbia.

1940   *Statistical Mechanics*, a book co-authored by Maria and Joe Mayer, is published.

1941   The Japanese bomb Pearl Harbor on December 7; Maria is offered a paid part-time teaching position at Sarah Lawrence College in Bronxville, New York.

1942   Joe begins working at the Aberdeen Proving Grounds in Maryland, testing military equipment; Maria joins the Substitute Alloy Materials (SAM) project and teaches at Sarah Lawrence College (until 1945).

1943   Leaves Sarah Lawrence for Columbia to conduct war research.

1945   The United States drops atomic bombs on Hiroshima and Nagasaki in August; in September, Maria and Joe are offered faculty positions at the University of Chicago.

1946   Becomes an associate professor at the University of Chicago; becomes a senior physicist at Argonne National Laboratory.

1948   Publishes a paper in *Physical Review* in April explaining her theory of the shell model of the atomic nucleus.

1955   *Elementary Theory of Nuclear Shell Structure*, co-authored by Maria Goeppert Mayer and Hans Jensen, is published.

1959   Maria and Joe accept posts at the University of California's new San Diego campus; too late, Chicago offers a full professorship, too. Maria suffers a stroke.

1963   In November, is awarded a share of the Nobel Prize in Physics, with Jensen and Eugene Wigner.

1972   Dies on February 20 at the age of 65.

Bibliography

Dash, Joan. *A Life of One's Own: Three Gifted Women and the Men They Married.* Paragon House, 1973.

———. *The Triumph of Discovery: Women Scientists Who Won the Nobel Prize.* Simon and Schuster, 1991.

Gabor, Andrea. *Einstein's Wife: Work and Marriage in the Lives of Five Great Twentieth-Century Women.* Viking, 1995.

Sachs, Robert G. "A Biographical Memoir: Maria Goeppert Mayer." *Biographical Memoirs,* vol. 50. National Academy of Sciences, 1979.

Eisenhart, Margaret A., and Elizabeth Finkel. *Women's Science: Learning from the Margins.* University of Chicago Press, 1998.

Hall, Mary Harrington. "The Nobel Genius." *San Diego Magazine,* August 1964.

Hawking, Stephen, ed. *On the Shoulders of Giants: The Great Works of Physics and Astronomy.* Running Press, 2002.

Herken, Greg. *Brotherhood of the Bomb: The Tangled Lives and Loyalties of Robert Oppenheimer, Ernest Lawrence, and Edward Teller.* Henry Holt, 2002.

McGrayne, Sharon Bertsch. *Nobel Prize Women in Science.* Birch Lane Press, 1995.

Phillips, Patricia. *The Scientific Lady: A Social History of Women's Scientific Interests, 1520–1918.* Weidenfeld and Nicolson, 1990.

Rhodes, Richard. *The Making of the Atomic Bomb.* Simon and Schuster, 1986.

Rossiter, Margaret W. *Women Scientists in America: Struggles and Strategies to 1940.* Johns Hopkins University Press, 1982.

————. *Women Scientists in America: Before Affirmative Action, 1940–1972.* Johns Hopkins University Press, 1995.

Serber, Robert. *The Los Alamos Primer: The First Lectures on How to Build an Atomic Bomb,* ed. Richard Rhodes. University of California Press, 1992.

Teller, Edward. *Memoirs: A Twentieth-Century Journey in Science and Politics.* Perseus Books, 2001.

Websites

Argonne National Laboratory: AIM System: Maria Goeppert Mayer
www.ipd.anl.gov/library/internet/mgm.html
Contains a complete list of Mayer's publications.

Professor S.A. Moszkowski's *Maria Goeppert Mayer Homepage*
www.physics.ucla.edu/~moszkows/mgm/mgmhmpg.htm
Moszkowski was a graduate student of Mayer.

The Nobel Prize in Physics, 1963
www.nobel.se/physics/laureates/1963/index.html

PhysicsWeb
www.physicsweb.org

A Science Odyssey: You Try It: Atom Builder
www.pbs.org/wgbh/aso/tryit/atom/

How Stuff Works: How Atoms Work
www.howstuffworks.com/atom.htm

City of Göttingen, Germany
www.eng.goettingen.de

The Association for Women in Science
1200 New York Ave., Suite 650 NW
Washington, DC USA 20005
202.326.8940
www.awis.org

Index

Index

Index

Picture Credits

Contributors

JOSEPH P. FERRY is a veteran journalist who has worked for several newspapers in the Philadelphia area since 1977. He has also written about actress Helen Hunt and actor/director Rob Reiner for Chelsea House. Mr. Ferry, a graduate of West Catholic High School for Boys and of Eastern College, lives in Perkasie, Pennsylvania with his wife, three children, and two dogs.

JILL SIDEMAN, PH.D. serves as vice president of CH2M HILL, an international environmental-consulting firm based in San Francisco. She was among the few women to study physical chemistry and quantum mechanics in the late 1960s and conducted over seven years of post-doctoral research in high-energy physics and molecular biology. In 1974, she co-founded a woman-owned environmental-consulting firm that became a major force in environmental-impact analysis, wetlands and coastal zone management, and energy conservation. She went on to become Director of Environmental Planning and Senior Client Service Manager at CH2M HILL. An active advocate of women in the sciences, she was elected in 2001 as president of the Association for Women in Science, a national organization "dedicated to achieving equity and full participation for women in science, mathematics, engineering and technology."